C000001579

EPHESIANS

your Identity in Christ

TONY MERIDA

LIFEWAY PRESS®
NASHVILLE, TENNESSEE

LifeWay | Students

Published by LifeWay Press®
© 2016 Tony Merida
Reprinted Feb. 2017, Aug. 2017, July 2018, Oct. 2018, June 2019, Aug. 2019, Oct. 2019

ISBN: 978-1-4300-6547-0
Item number: 005792204

Dewey Decimal Classification Number: 248.83
Subject Heading: RELIGION \ CHRISTIAN MINISTRY \ YOUTH

Printed in the United States of America

Student Ministry Publishing
LifeWay Resources
One LifeWay Plaza
Nashville, TN 37234

We believe that the Bible has God for its author; salvation for its end;
and truth, without any mixture of error, for its matter
and that all Scripture is totally true and trustworthy.
To review LifeWay's doctrinal guideline,
please visit www.lifeway.com/doctrinalguideline.

Table of CONTENTS

MEET THE AUTHORS //

TONY MERIDA is the founding pastor of Imago Dei Church in Raleigh, North Carolina. He also serves as an associate professor of preaching at Southeastern Baptist Theological Seminary in Wake Forest, North Carolina. He's the author of several books, including *Ordinary: How to Turn the World Upside Down*.

//

BEN REED adapted Tony Merida's study of the Book of Ephesians for small groups. Ben is the lead small-groups pastor at the Lake Forest campus of Saddleback Church in Orange County, California. Having led small-group ministries at a variety of different churches, he thrives on building healthy, biblical, authentic, life-changing communities.

A LETTER FROM TONY //

Hey Students!

I hope you enjoy studying the Book of Ephesians. I told my wife that I want to take our kids through this study. (We have three in middle school and two in high school). So, we'll be walking through these pages with you.

There's really nothing more important than knowing your identity in Christ. I pray that this study will help you learn what it means to be "in Christ" and how to live a life that glorifies Him. You're in the midst of a very challenging, but important, time in your lives.

I have written this study so that you will center your lives on Jesus, and live out of an overflow of love for Him. If you love Jesus deeply, it will impact your whole life dramatically. So go for it. Be all in. Give yourself to Jesus and His cause. He's the only One who can satisfy your soul and fulfill your longing for identity, community, and meaning.

—Tony

INTRO //

Many of us struggle to find our identity, thinking we can search the world and find it. When we don't make the team or make an A, we spiral into an emotional wasteland. When our friend groups change, we freak out. When someone questions whether the talent we're reputed to be good at is truly good, we're shaken to our core.

The Book of Ephesians has an abundance of wisdom to share with us that will reveal where our identity should be anchored. When we anchor our identity in Christ, the shifting winds of change that inevitably happen in life won't sink our ship.

Over the next six weeks we'll look at these topics from Ephesians:

1. "The Struggle in Ephesus": where our identity is centered

2. "New Life in Christ": our identity reconciled with God

3. "New Life in Community": our identity reconciled with people

4. "Pursuing Unity in Christ": our identity unified in the local church

5. "Pursuing Holiness in Christ": how our identity shapes our behavior

6. "Be Strong in Christ": the war against our identity

My prayer is that everyone will dig deeply into the truths of Scripture as we pursue honesty with ourselves and our small groups. The more we're vulnerable with our weaknesses, the closer and safer our groups will become. The closer and safer our groups become, the healthier we'll become, and the more we'll begin living in the freedom and strength of our identity in Christ.

HOW TO USE ////////////////////

This Bible study book includes six weeks of content. Each week has an introductory page summarizing the focus of the week's study, followed by content designed for groups and individuals.

Group Sessions

Regardless of the day of the week your group meets, each week of content begins with the group session. This group session is designed to be one hour or more, with approximately 15 to 20 minutes of teaching and 45 minutes of personal interaction. It's even better if your group is able to meet longer than an hour, allowing more time for participants to interact with one another.

Each group session uses the following format to facilitate simple yet meaningful interaction among group members, with God's Word, and with the video teaching.

> **START**
This page includes questions to get the conversation started and to introduce the video segment.

> **WATCH**
This page includes key points from the video teaching, along with space for taking notes as participants watch the video.

> **DISCUSS**
These two pages include questions and statements that guide the group to respond to the video teaching and to relevant Bible passages.

> **PRAY**
This final page of each group session includes a prompt for a closing time of prayer together and space for recording prayer requests of group members.

Individual Discovery

This small-group resource provides individuals with optional activities during the week, appealing to different learning styles, schedules, and levels of engagement. These options include a plan for application and accountability, a Scripture-reading plan with journaling prompts, a devotion, and two personal studies.

⟩ THIS WEEK'S PLAN

Immediately following the group session's prayer page is a weekly plan offering guidance for everyone to engage with that week's focal point, regardless of a person's maturity level or that week's schedule.

You can choose to take advantage of some or all of the options provided. Those options are divided into three categories.

⟩ READ

A daily reading plan is outlined for Scriptures related to the group session. Space for personal notes is also provided. Instructions for using the H.E.A.R. journaling method for reading Scripture can be found on pages 8–11.

⟩ REFLECT

A one-page devotional option is provided each week to help members reflect on a biblical truth related to the group session.

⟩ PERSONAL STUDY

Two personal studies are provided each week to take individuals deeper into Scripture and to supplement the biblical truths introduced in the teaching time. These pages challenge individuals to grow in their understanding of God's Word and to make practical applications to their lives.

H.E.A.R. METHOD OF JOURNALING /////////////////////////////

DAILY BIBLE READING

This Bible study includes a daily reading plan for each week. Making time in a busy schedule to focus on God through His Word is a vital part of the Christian life. If you're unable to do anything else provided in your Bible study book during a certain week, try to spend a few minutes in God's Word. The verse selections will take you deeper into stories and concepts that support the teaching and discussion during that week's group session.

WHY DO YOU NEED A PLAN?

When you're a new believer or at various other times in your life, you may find yourself in a place where you don't know where to begin reading your Bible or how to personally approach Scripture. You may have tried the open-and-point method, in which you simply opened your Bible and pointed to a verse, hoping to get something out of the random selection from God's Word. Reading random Scriptures won't provide solid biblical growth any more then eating random food from your pantry will provide solid physical growth.

An effective plan must be well balanced for healthy growth. When it comes to reading the Bible, well balanced and effective mean reading and applying. A regular habit is great, but simply checking a box off your task list when you've completed your daily reading isn't enough. Knowing more about God is also great, but simply reading for spiritual knowledge still isn't enough. You also want to respond to what you're reading by taking action as you listen to what God is saying. After all, it's God's Word.

To digest more of the Word, this study not only provides a weekly reading plan but also encourage you to use a simplified version of the *H.E.A.R.* journaling method. (If this method advances your personal growth, check out *Foundations: A 260-Day Bible-Reading Plan for Busy Believers* by Robby and Kandi Gallaty.)

JOURNALING WHAT YOU HEAR IN GOD'S WORD

You may or may not choose to keep a separate journal in addition to the space provided in this book. A separate journal would provide extra space as well as the opportunity to continue your journal after this study is completed. The H.E.A.R. journaling method promotes reading the Bible with a life-transforming purpose. You'll read in order to understand and respond to God's Word.

The H.E.A.R. acronym stands for *Highlight, Explain, Apply*, and *Respond*. Each of these four steps creates an atmosphere for hearing God speak. After settling on a reading plan, like the one provided in this book in the section "Read" each week, establish a time for studying God's Word.

BEFORE YOU BEGIN: THE MOST IMPORTANT STEP

Always begin your time with prayer. Pause and sincerely ask God to speak to you. It's absolutely imperative that you seek God's guidance in order to understand His Word (1 Cor. 2:12-14). Every time you open your Bible, pray a simple prayer like the one David prayed: "Open my eyes so that I may contemplate wonderful things from Your instruction" (Ps. 119:18).

〉 **H = HIGHLIGHT**

After praying for the Holy Spirit's guidance, open this book to the week's reading plan, open a journal if you'd like more space than this book provides, and open your Bible. For an illustration let's assume you're reading Philippians 4:10-13. Verse 13 may speak to you as something you want to remember, so you'd simply highlight that verse in your Bible.

If keeping a H.E.A.R. journal, on the top line write the Scripture reference and the date, and make up a title to summarize the meaning of the passage. Then write the letter *H* and record the verse that stood out and that you highlighted in your

Bible. This practice will make it easy to look back through your journal to find a passage you want to revisit in the future.

> ## E = EXPLAIN

After you've highlighted your verse(s), explain what the text means. How would you summarize this passage in your own words? By asking some simple questions, with the help of the Holy Spirit, you can understand the meaning of the passage or verse. (A good study Bible can help answer more in-depth questions as you learn to explain a passage of Scripture.) Here are a few good questions to get you started:

> Why was the verse or passage written?

> To whom was it originally written?

> How does the verse or passage fit with the verses before and after it?

> Why would the Holy Spirit include this passage in the Bible book?

> What does God intend to communicate through the text?

If keeping a H.E.A.R. journal, below the *H* write the letter *E* and explain the text in your own words. Record any answers to questions that help you understand the passage of Scripture.

> ## A = APPLY

At this point you're beginning the process of discovering the specific personal word God has for you from His Word. What's important is that you're engaging with the text and wrestling with the meaning. Application is the heart of the process. Everything you've done so far combines under this heading. As you've done before, answer a series of questions to discover the significance of these verses to you personally. Ask yourself:

> How can this verse or passage help me?

⟩ What's God saying to me?

⟩ What would the application of this verse look like in my life?

These questions bridge the gap between the ancient world and your world today. They provide a way for God to speak to you through the specific passage or verse.

If keeping a H.E.A.R. journal, write the letter *A* under the letter *E*, where you wrote a short summary explaining the text. Challenge yourself to write between two and five sentences about the way the text applies to your life.

⟩ R = RESPOND

Finally, you'll respond to the text. A personal response may take on many forms. You may write an action step, describe a change in perspective, or simply respond in prayer to what you've learned. For example, you may ask for help in being bold or generous, you may need to repent of unconfessed sin, or you may want to praise God. Keep in mind that you're responding to what you've just read.

In this book or in your journal, record your personal application of each passage of Scripture. You may want to write a brief explanation-and-application summary: *"The verse means _____, so I can or will _____."*

If keeping a H.E.A.R. journal, write the letter *R*, along with the way you'll respond to what you highlighted, explained, and applied.

Notice that all the words in the H.E.A.R. method are action words: Highlight, Explain, Apply, Respond. God doesn't want us to sit back and wait for Him to drop truth into our laps. God wants us to actively pursue Him instead of waiting passively. Jesus said:

Keep asking, and it will be given to you. Keep searching, and you will find. Keep knocking, and the door will be opened to you.

Matthew 7:7

SESSION

1

THE STRUGGLE IN EPHESUS

Ephesians contains only six chapters. It's a mere 155 verses. If you read it straight through, it would take you about 20 minutes. Yet the rich wisdom packed in this book will take you much longer than 20 minutes to apply and live out. If you want to use what you learn from this book, read it slowly. And often.

Paul, the author, wrote to the people in Ephesus by starting out with a few seemingly insignificant statements. A reader could easily gloss over these words in an attempt to get to "the important stuff." But if you do that, you'll regret it. By overlooking even some of the words here, you may short-circuit the work God wants to do in your heart instead of digging deep into who God declared you to be. And who God declared you to be is more powerful than who you feel you are.

The One you fix your eyes on is both the source and the object of your identity.

When you get the focus right, you'll gain a lot from this study.

start

Spend a few minutes hanging out and getting to know your group.

Use the following content to begin your time together.

When you were a kid, what did you want to be when you grew up?

How have your goals and dreams changed over the last few years?

As kids, we dream. We dream of one day playing professional sports, traveling the universe as an astronaut, or being a superhero who can fly. Maybe you still have some pretty big dreams.

Deep down we have a desire to do something significant and make a difference in the world. And there's nothing wrong with that desire. There's actually something God-honoring in it. The hero or heroine's story touches us deeply because God has wired us for significance. The deeper questions we all have to answer are about what defines who we are and where we'll find our significance.

In this first session, Tony Merida will introduce us to the Book of Ephesians by starting where Paul started the letter: defining our identity.

Before you watch the video for Session 1, pray that God will speak to your group through what you learn today.

watch

Use the space below to follow along and take notes as you watch the video for Session 1.

1. If your _____ is not in Christ, you will be dissatisfied. You were made for a relationship with God through Christ.

2. When you become a _____, you become a new person. You get a completely new identity.

3. We have to keep feeding our souls with _____.

4. Are you enjoying the _____ of being in Christ?

5. You need your _____ to be enthralled with the Person and work of Jesus Christ.

6. If you love Jesus deeply, it will change your _____ dramatically.

Scripture: Ephesians 1:1-2

Discuss

Use the following statements and questions to discuss the video.

The most basic yet important question you can ask yourself right now is "Am I in Christ?" The Book of Ephesians is an amazing place to discover who Jesus is and who He has created you to be.

> **How have you seen a friend's behavior change when he or she started a new relationship?**

> **How does your relationship with Jesus affect the way you live your life?**

> **If you've been following Jesus for a number of years, how have things changed since you first came to know Him?**

Read aloud Ephesians 1:1-2.

Paul, an apostle, wrote this book and began his greeting with the words "Grace to you and peace …" (v. 2).

> **How does knowing that you're covered in grace and peace affect the way you see yourself?**

When we read the Bible, we may feel there's a huge gap between the lives of the people in Scripture and our lives. But the culture Paul described in the Book of Ephesians is oddly similar to ours today.

> **In what things (for example: activities, behaviors, friendships, personalities) does culture tell us to find our identity?**

> **According to the video and Tony's teaching from Acts 19 (about Paul's time in Ephesus), what did the apostle Paul do in an effort to change the culture in Ephesus (v. 10)? What happened as a result?**

How should living in the reality of a new identity change the way you:

get along with others at school and church?

respond when others criticize you?

view success and popularity?

spend your summer vacation?

It's easy to see following God as a relationship that limits what we are "allowed" to do in life. As you read the Bible, you see the Ten Commandments and a bunch of other rules that keep you from doing things. You may be tempted to say, "I wish God would let me …" But the reality is that being followers of Jesus and rooting our identity in Him provides us many privileges.

As a follower of Christ, whose identity is rooted in Him, what privileges do you have that others don't?

As we dive in to this first week's study, you may have some doubts. Or excitement. Or questions.

What are your hopes or expectations for this study of Ephesians?

We all have hopes and expectations in starting this study. God has hopes and expectations for us too.

Conclude your group time with the prayer activity on the next page. Then, complete the personal study for Session 1 before your next meeting.

Pray

The good news of the gospel is that our identity is found in Christ—knowing Him and being in Him. If we want to live in light of our identity in Christ, then we have to understand that identity.

Before we go any further, let's stop and pray.

Ask for prayer requests for those who need grace and peace this week.

Spend a few minutes praying for each person in the group. Then, ask God to show up and speak clearly to each person during the next six weeks.

Prayer Requests

This Week's Plan

WORSHIP

> Read your Bible. Complete the reading plan on page 20.

> Spend time with God by engaging with the devotional experience on page 21.

> Connect with God every day in prayer.

PERSONAL STUDY

> Read and interact with "You're a Saint!" on page 22.

> Read and interact with "Don't Lose Your First Love" on page 26.

APPLICATION

> Identify an area of your life in which you need grace and peace (Eph. 1:2).

> Memorize Ephesians 1:2: "Grace to you and peace from God our Father and the Lord Jesus Christ."

> Connect with someone in your group this week to talk more about your thoughts on this week's study and your expectations for the group going forward.

> Start a journal. This week record 10 things in which you've rooted your identity, other than Jesus, throughout your life. Based on the discussion in this week's group session, record 10 truths that would disprove those false identities.

Read

Read through the following Scripture this week. Use the H. E. A. R. acronym in the space provided to help you as you record your thoughts or action steps.

Day 1: Ephesians 1

Day 2: Ephesians 2

Day 3: Ephesians 3

Day 4: Ephesians 4

Day 5: Ephesians 5

Day 6: Ephesians 6

Day 7: Ephesians 2

Reflect

TWO IDENTIFIABLE IDENTITY TRUTHS

Did you know you can buy identity-theft insurance? If someone steals your identity, you have a backup plan. You have security in knowing that if your identity is stolen, you can recover your losses with minimal damage and reclaim your lost identity.

Thankfully, our true identity in Christ is secure. Read these passages:

> *To all who did receive him, to those who believed in his name, he gave the right to become children of God.*
>
> *John 1:12 (NIV)*

> *Accept one another, then, just as Christ accepted you, in order to bring praise to God.*
>
> *Romans 15:7 (NIV)*

Notice two key truths about our identity from these verses:

> When we receive Christ, we become children of God.

> Our acceptance of others isn't based on their actions. It's based on Christ's acceptance of us.

As children of God, we receive all the family benefits: unconditional love, safety, provision, guidance, and much more. As brothers and sisters in Christ, we accept others regardless of how they've treated us, because God has loved us regardless of how we've treated Him. What amazing freedom is that?

Reflect on both of these truths. Which do you need to apply right now?

Personal study 1

YOU'RE A SAINT!

Impersonating someone else is nothing new.

You may have discussed this in the group session. Kids dress up as superheroes, princesses, soldiers, monsters, or grown-ups. Imagination is fun, and imitation is natural.

There's a danger when we try to impersonate others' identities with our faith, though. Read these words from another of Paul's letters:

> I appeal to you, brothers, by the name of our Lord Jesus Christ, that all of you agree, and that there be no divisions among you, but that you be united in the same mind and the same judgment. For it has been reported to me by Chloe's people that there is quarreling among you, my brothers. What I mean is that each one of you says, "I follow Paul," or "I follow Apollos," or "I follow Cephas," or "I follow Christ."
>
> 1 Corinthians 1:10-12

Circle the activities Paul wants us to do, according to this passage.

Underline the dangers he warned against.

In Ephesians 1, Paul used a carefully chosen noun when he addressed the people to whom he wrote his letter. Check it out:

> Paul, an apostle of Christ Jesus by the will of God, To the saints who are in Ephesus, and are faithful in Christ Jesus.
>
> Ephesians 1:1

While we're off somewhere trying to root our faith in the faith of others by identifying with a certain belief camp or "celebrity" preacher, Paul called us saints. *Saints!* Let that sink into your heart for a moment. (Also notice that Paul used the same word in 1:15,18; 3:8,18; 4:12; 5:3; 6:18.)

Be honest. When you think of a saint, who comes to mind?

What have those people done or how did they live to make you think of them and list their names?

Did you include yourself in that list? Why or why not?

The word *saint* finds its roots in the Old Testament, where God chose a people to be set apart from the other nations, to be His holy people. Now Christ has made us into His holy people (Eph. 5:25b-27). We are holy, not because of what we've done, but because of what Christ has done. In other words, you're not a saint because you've lived a perfect life. You're a saint because Jesus did live a perfect life, and you've placed your faith in Him!

How does being called a saint give you comfort and security?

What responsibilities do you feel that you have, now that you know you're a saint?

To be a saint means to "be in Christ," or to be in union with Christ. "This phrase occurs some 164 times in Paul's 13 epistles."[1] Being in Christ is a central theme in Paul's writings, and it should be a central theme in our lives. We're united with Christ in His death, as well as in His resurrection (Eph. 2:5-7). To be in Christ doesn't mean you're inside Him; it means you're one with Him in the same way your arm is a part of your body. When you're in Christ, your desires are satisfied (John 6:35). And we can rest eternally at peace, knowing we can't be snatched out of his hand (John 10:28-30). We're protected. We're secure.

But one thing being in Christ doesn't give us is a lack of opposition. In fact, it may increase opposition. Satan would love nothing more than to destroy someone who's in Christ and seek to break that union apart. If he can get a saint to fall, he will get others to fall with them. A saint is like the first domino in the row.

Though we may be surrounded by opposition on every side, and though we may fall, our eternal identity is secure:

> *All that the Father gives me will come to me, and whoever comes to me I will never cast out.*
>
> *John 6:37*

1. Tony Merida, *Christ-Centered Exposition Commentary: Exalting Jesus in Ephesus* (Nashville: B&H, 2014), 13.

List ways you feel opposition, even though you know your identity is secure.

List ways being united with Christ provides you with confidence to stand strong against opposition.

Close your study time in prayer, asking God to remind you of your sainthood every day.

Personal study 2

DON'T LOSE YOUR FIRST LOVE

Paul's letter to the Ephesians isn't the only book of the Bible addressed to that particular church. We read another account in Scripture about the people in Ephesus: Jesus had a word of correction and encouragement for them in the Book of Revelation:

> I know your works, your toil and your patient endurance, and how you cannot bear with those who are evil, but have tested those who call themselves apostles and are not, and found them to be false. I know you are enduring patiently and bearing up for my name's sake, and you have not grown weary. But I have this against you, that you have abandoned the love you had at first.
>
> Revelation 2:2-4

This passage identifies three character qualities these people possessed, revealing a level of countercultural identity we don't often see today.

What positive traits were the Ephesians known for?

1.

2.

3.

Jesus said, "I know" (v. 2). What thoughts or feelings do you have when you read that Jesus was fully aware of everything—good and bad—in the Ephesians' lives?

What would you have done differently yesterday when you consider the fact that Jesus knows everything about your heart and actions?

As countercultural as the Ephesians' admirable qualities were, Jesus also had something against these people.

What did Jesus have against the Ephesians?

How would you describe the tone of Jesus' words *against* and *abandoned* in verse 4?

What was Jesus' point when He listed several positive qualities but identified one problem?

What does Jesus' emphasis reveal about the significance of love?

One of the saddest verses in all of Scripture is this: "You have abandoned the love you had at first" (v. 4). If they abandoned a first love, this means they once had a first love. They were in love with Jesus, but along the way their affections had shifted.

Think about the relationship you have with your best friend. You two have been friends for most of your lives, and you love your best friend. In fact, you could even say you are closer than you've ever been. You and your best friend have had your share of bumps along the way, but in each season, you have worked hard to keep your friendship strong. You've chosen to love each other, no matter what. The danger isn't that you'll randomly abandon each other one day. It's that your love will fade over time. If you and your friend stop intentionally building your relationship, your "first love" will slide into something much less. Even though everything may seem fine on the outside, when our hearts become disengaged, love begins to fade.

Our faith can do the same thing.

In your relationship with God, when have you abandoned your first love? What drew your heart away from Him?

In what parts of your life are you most tempted to be motivated by something other than the love of Christ?

Who in your life can help ensure that you don't slowly drift, backslide, or lose your genuine love for Christ?

Read Psalm 51.

Now let's look specifically at verses 10-12:

> *Create in me a clean heart, O God, and renew a right spirit within me. Cast me not away from your presence, and take not your Holy Spirit from me. Restore to me the joy of your salvation, and uphold me with a willing spirit.*
>
> *Psalm 51:10-12*

Why did the psalmist need his joy to be restored?

What did he ask God to do to restore it?

When have you needed to ask God to restore your joy? How did He give you back the joy of His salvation?

It's possible for anyone to lose their love for Jesus. It rarely happens overnight, but over a series of events and seasons of life, our love fades. When this happens, it's not the time to throw up our hands in frustration. It's the time for spiritual renewal! The antidote for losing your love is to fall in love again.

Since you're just beginning this study, take the temperature of where you are in your relationship with God. Ask Him to meet you exactly where you are and to give you grace to grow as you fall more deeply in love with Him.

SESSION

2

NEW LIFE IN CHRIST

Knowing where we came from is important to understanding who we are, what we desire, and what makes us tick.

In order to understand our new identity, we've got to uncover our old identity. We've got to dig deeper into who we were, beyond our history and immediate family, to see the ugly truth. Paul shows us an unfiltered picture of who we really are.

But light shines the brightest against a dark canvas. This week, we are headed toward a beacon of bright, shining hope. This identity-shaping hope drives us toward action.

Ephesians 2:1-10 will help us clearly see three things:

> What do we need to be saved from?

> How are we saved?

> What is the result?

The way you answer these questions will shape the way you live your life.

start

Use the following content to begin your time together.

What truths did you discover through the reading, reflection, or personal study this week? Which personal study ("You're a Saint!" or "Don't Lose Your First Love") resonated most deeply with you? Why?

How did you apply the truths to your life?

During group session 1, you were encouraged to think through ways your life is different because of Jesus. As you reflected on that question this past week, what other aspects of your life came to mind?

In this week's video, Tony will walk us through Ephesians 2:1-10 as we dive deeper into who we were before Jesus, and the new life we are given through His death. We'll see how our identity is radically formed through the greatest gift we've ever been given.

Pray for God to open your hearts and minds before you watch the video for Session 2.

watch

Use the space below to follow along and take notes as you watch video session 2.

1. Apart from Christ, we are spiritually _____.

2. We were _____ of God.

3. Jesus has become our substitute, and now we have _____.

4. This passage should compel us to _____. No one is beyond the reach of God's amazing grace.

5. This text should encourage us to _____.

6. The text inspires us to _____. We want to work for the Savior.

Scripture: Ephesians 2:1-10

Answers: 1. dead 2. enemies 3. life 4. hope 5. worship 6. work

Discuss

Use the following statements and questions to discuss the video.

More likely than not, you don't like to think of yourself as an enemy of God. But as Tony explained while looking at Ephesians 2, that's exactly what we were before Jesus.

Read Ephesians 2:1-3:

In this passage Paul used the phrase, "Among whom we all...like the rest of mankind" (v. 3). Nobody is exempt from the truth that, apart from Christ, we are dead. *Nobody.*

Why is it so significant that Paul referred to us as "dead" people?

Paul was not saying that you (before Christ) were as bad as you could be. You could have acted much worse than you did. You may have even done some "good" deeds! What Paul was saying, though, is that without Christ as your King, without having been reborn a new creature in Christ, your motives and actions couldn't ultimately please God. (See Rom. 8:8.) And because you were cut off from the source of all life: God himself.

Dead things can't make themselves alive. So, if we were dead, then we need to be made alive.

Read Ephesians 2:4-7.

> *God, being rich in mercy, because of the great love with which he loved us, even when we were dead in our trespasses, made us alive together with Christ—by grace you have been saved— and raised us up with him and seated us with him in the heavenly places in Christ Jesus, so that in the coming ages he might show the immeasurable riches of his grace in kindness toward us in Christ Jesus.*
>
> *Ephesians 2:4-7*

Tony says, "Works matter to the Christian, but we're not working for salvation, we're working from salvation." The words *for* and *from* are subtle, but incredibly important. The apostle Paul chose his words carefully.

If our works don't save us, then what's their purpose?

Read Ephesians 2:8-9.

Why is it vital to know that salvation is a gift, not a prize?

Tony walks through a short list of other religions, mentioning how Christianity is different than all other world religions.

What makes Christianity distinct among all word religions and philosophies?

How would you explain the "good news" of the gospel?

It's important to not only know who you are in Christ, but to also be able to share the good news of how Christ has given you a new identity.

1. **Who were you before you came to know Christ?**

2. **How did you come to faith in Christ? Name a few people who influenced you.**

3. **How are you different now? Name two or three events that have been significant in your spiritual life.**

Conclude the session with the prayer activity on the following page.

Pray

The good news of the gospel is that we were once dead, but God, in His grace and mercy, has made us alive in Christ! Take a couple of minutes to read and think about your answers to the following questions. Answer these questions on your own, then share with the group if you're comfortable.

Who do you know who needs to hear the good news? Record their names or initials here.

When are you going to see, or communicate with, them this week?

How are you going to share hope and truth with them?

Pray for two things:

> **One of your group members by name**

> **The person (or initials) they shared specifically**

To build in accountability, reach out to the group member you're praying for this week. Check in to see how they're doing, and if they've had a chance to talk with the person God placed on their heart.

Pray for the opportunities you'll each have, and that God would open up the hearts of those people with whom we will come in contact.

Prayer Requests

This Week's Plan

WORSHIP

> Read your Bible. Complete the reading plan on page 38.

> Spend time with God by engaging with the devotional experience on page 39.

> Connect with God every day in prayer.

PERSONAL STUDY

> Read and interact with "Dead Men Tell No Tales" on page 40.

> Read and interact with "United with Christ" on page 44.

APPLICATION

> Identify an area of your life that needs to change as a result of the truth you learned in this session.

> Memorize Ephesians 2:8-9: "For by grace you have been saved through faith. And this is not your own doing; it is the gift of God, not a result of works, so that no one may boast."

> Connect with someone in your group this week to talk more about your thoughts on this week's study and your expectations for the group going forward.

> Continue your journal. This week, write out how the truths of the gospel inform your daily life and how you see God at work.

Read

Read through the following Scripture this week. Use the space provided to jot down your thoughts and responses.

Day 1: Ephesians 1

Day 2: Ephesians 2

Day 3: Ephesians 3

Day 4: Ephesians 4

Day 5: Ephesians 5

Day 6: Ephesians 6

Day 7: Ephesians 2

Reflect

WHO NEEDS RADICAL GRACE?

You were given radical grace—so radical that it raised dead things. Namely, *you.*

Grace is something given to us by God that we didn't, and can't, deserve. Read what Paul wrote to the Christians in Ephesus.

> *God, being rich in mercy, because of the great love with which he loved us, even when we were dead in our trespasses, made us alive together with Christ—by grace you have been saved.*
>
> *Ephesians 2:4-5*

God never gave up on you.

Not even when you were dead in sin.

He gave you salvation and new life in Christ.

So don't lose hope. Not on your circumstances. And not on other people. God is still in the business of bringing the dead to life.

What in your life feels dead or hopeless and needs God's radical grace to bring new life?

Journal a short prayer to God, asking Him to do what only He can do.

Personal study 1

DEAD MEN TELL NO TALES

Death is a topic we don't like to talk about. When we talk about death with others, we soften the language by using phrases like, "He passed away," or, "She's no longer with us." Nobody likes going into a funeral home. The sights, colors, and smells stay with us long after we've left.

We don't like to talk about the death of anything. It's painful to talk about the death of a dream or the death of a relationship. We don't even like it when our phones die. But, when it comes to our spiritual lives, the Bible describes us as "dead" apart from Christ.

Read what Paul wrote about spiritual death in Romans 8:6-8.

> *To set the mind on the flesh is death, but to set the mind on the Spirit is life and peace. For the mind that is set on the flesh is hostile to God, for it does not submit to God's law; indeed, it cannot. Those who are in the flesh cannot please God.*
>
> *Romans 8:6-8*

How do you think we can go about setting our minds "on the Spirit"?

What are some daily activities you can do to wage war on your flesh?

Renewing our minds is a supernatural act. There are activities we can and should do, but ultimately, we rely on the Holy Spirit to change our hearts and minds.

Read what Paul wrote about spiritual transformation in Romans 12:1-2.

> *I appeal to you therefore, brothers, by the mercies of God, to present your bodies as a living sacrifice, holy and acceptable to God, which is your spiritual worship. Do not be conformed to this world, but be transformed by the renewal of your mind, that by testing you may discern what is the will of God, what is good and acceptable and perfect.*
>
> *Romans 12:1-2*

A "living sacrifice" is an oxymoron—it shouldn't be possible. A sacrifice is something that has died and is presented as an offering. Yet, this is precisely how Paul describes us.

If a "living sacrifice" is "your spiritual worship," how would you describe "worship"? Write a definition in your own words.

The words "conformed" and "transformed" are contrasting terms. To be conformed is a passive state, where people, circumstances, and seasons are "conforming" you to themselves. To be "transformed" is to be changed, and this comes through a renewed mind. It's the difference between going downhill (conformed) and going uphill (transformed). Or another way to think about it is that it's the difference between swimming with the current (conformed) and swimming against the current (transformed). In our flesh, we naturally drift toward conformity. But when we are united with Christ, we are being transformed.

What time in your life did you feel yourself conforming to life around you? What was that like?

What time in your life did you feel yourself being transformed by Christ? What was that like?

According to this passage, we learn God's will for our lives by testing it out. Sometimes this happens individually. Sometimes this happens in community, as others who love us and want God's best for our lives confirm or deny God's leading in our lives.

If you want to know God's will for your life, how will you be intentional this week to test and discern what is good?

Transformation is possible. By God's grace we can be transformed from death to life. Our lives can become acts of worship as living sacrifices. We can wage war against the self-destructive desires of our flesh and set our minds on the goodness of our heavenly Father.

Read the parable of the prodigal son in Luke 15:11-32.

How did the father's reaction to his son's return line up with the way you think of God?

What was so wrong about the older brother's reaction?

When have you found yourself acting like the older brother?

Take a look at these words John Newton wrote in the late 1700s:

> Amazing grace! How sweet the sound
> That saved a wretch like me!
> I once was lost, but now am found;
> Was blind, but now I see.

Looking back on your life, when have you been most thankful for grace?

As you close in prayer, worship God. Praise Him for the life you have and the death you escaped.

Personal study 2

UNITED WITH CHRIST

To be united with Christ means that we are one with Him. Obviously. This should result in a changed life, right? If we are united with Christ in His death, burial, and resurrection, our lives should show evidence of that union. The Bible calls our changed life, and the new actions that result, "fruit."

Read what Paul wrote about spiritual fruit in Galatians 5:22-23.

> *The fruit of the Spirit is love, joy, peace, patience, kindness, goodness, faithfulness, gentleness, self-control; against such things there is no law.*
>
> *Galatians 5:22-23*

Notice the singular word: *fruit*. Not *fruits*. This is significant because the work of the Spirit when we are united with Christ should manifest itself as all of these things. We don't get to say, "I'm kind…that's my fruit. But I'm not patient…I don't have that fruit." If you are in Christ, you do have that fruit!

Which characteristic(s) are easiest for you?

Which are the most difficult?

Why do you think some are more difficult for you to live out?

Although we are "in Christ," we are also still living in our mortal bodies. Which means we mess up much more than we like.

There's something you did that you regret. Someone you hurt. Somewhere you went. Someone you trusted. You dropped all your money on something. You were hurt by someone.

Maybe your mistakes were made public, your life on display as a spectacle for others. Maybe someone else's stupid decisions affected you. And you'd like your mistake to cancel out her choices, too.

What have you done that you're ashamed of?

Who have you confessed that to?

The good news about being in Christ is that God removes the guilt and shame from us.

Read Psalm 103:8-12.

> *The LORD is merciful and gracious,*
> *slow to anger and abounding in steadfast love.*
> *He will not always chide,*
> *nor will he keep his anger forever.*
> *He does not deal with us according to our sins,*
> *nor repay us according to our iniquities.*
> *For as high as the heavens are above the earth,*
> *so great is his steadfast love toward those who fear him;*
> *as far as the east is from the west,*
> *so far does he remove our transgressions from us.*
>
> *Psalm 103:8-12*

Circle the character traits of God that you see in this Psalm. Which of these traits do you need most right now? Why?

Do you know how far the east is from the west? Infinite. Because the east and the west never touch. Ever. East is never west, and west is never east. "As far as the east is from the west" means that God has completely removed your sin from you—it can't be further from you.

As you reflect on the painful choices you've made in life, how does knowing that God doesn't hold them against you make you feel?

To whom do you need to extend that same type of mercy?

David went on to say of God, in Psalm 103:13:

> *As a father shows compassion to his children,*
> *so the LORD shows compassion to those who fear him.*
>
> *Psalm 103:13*

A father doesn't hate his children who need a redo. He has compassion for them. We may hold on to our hurt, our despair, and our frustrations. We may cling to our past failures. But God offers "steadfast love" to us. He redeems us "from the pit" (Ps. 103:4). In fact, the moment we turn to God, we find Him running to us! (Refer back to Luke 15, mentioned in this week's Personal Study 1 on pages 42-43.) He's not standing ready to condemn us all over again. He's removed our sins from us.

To be united with Christ means we get to receive the glorious gift of compassion.

As you close this week's Personal Study, thank God that He has removed your sins from you. Ask Him to give you the strength to live life, not as a guilty criminal, but as a free child of the King.

3

NEW LIFE IN COMMUNITY

We all long to belong. Feeling left out cuts us to our core, because something deep inside of us wants to be known, accepted, and loved. And this isn't a bad thing! In fact, it's a God-given desire to be a part of a community of people that accepts us for who He created us to be.

This week's Scripture focuses on our pre-Christ, alienated state. As in previous sessions, we learned that we can't fully embrace the "good" until we lock eyes with the "bad." Again, as in previous sessions, we'll notice that our pre-Christ state is pretty bleak.

But Paul shows us that Christ's death was sufficient to reconcile us to one another, forming a community of people we now belong to.

If you've ever wished you were a part of a group you weren't invited to, or if you've ever felt "on the outside," this week's study will show you once and for all that Jesus died to fulfill that craving as He made us citizens of a new kingdom.

But the journey won't be easy. Any time you bring sinners in close proximity with sinners, challenges come up. Let's take some time and see what Ephesians 2 has to say about overcoming this reality to build healthy communities.

start

Use the following content to start your time together.

What truths did you discover through the reading, reflection, or personal study this week? How did you apply the truths to your life?

From the personal study, "United with Christ," which fruit did you struggle to live out this week? Where did you see growth?

We've learned the truth that Jesus died to reconcile us to God, and this week we'll dive into the truth that Jesus died to reconcile us to others. As important as it is for us to live at peace with God (our vertical relationship), it's vital for us to live at peace with others (our horizontal relationships). If that challenges you already, then good! Here we go!

Pray for God to open your hearts and minds before you watch the video for Session 3.

watch

Use the space below to follow along and take notes as you watch video Session 3.

1. It's the gospel that brings _____ groups of people together.

2. If you're in Christ, not only do you have a new _____. You have a new _____.

3. We have a new _____.

4. We have new brothers and sisters. We are made part of the _____ of God.

5. You're _____ of the kingdom of God.

6. We're a _____.

Scripture: Ephesians 2:11-22

Answers: 1. different 2. identity, community 3. Father 4. household 5. citizens 6. temple

Discuss

When we think of rivalries, it's easy to think of sports teams or political parties. It's easy because of how quickly they come to mind, and because they tend to operate outside of us. Maybe we don't have to look our rivals in the eye every week. It becomes more personal when your rival is across the room from you.

Have you ever met a difficult person? What made this person so difficult?

Read Ephesians 2:11-12.

Paul described us as "separated from Christ, alienated." What does it mean to be alienated from someone?

Whom do you feel alienated from in this season of life?

What would reconciliation look like for you?

In verses 11-12, Paul tells us that we were apart from Christ, separated from God, and without hope. It's really a bleak picture. But an amazing change is described in verse 13.

Read Ephesians 2:13-14.

Christ's blood is the bridge that brings us near, though we were far off.

What's significant about "the blood of Christ"?

Based on this passage, what should we do when there's a wall between us and someone else?

Read Ephesians 2:19-22.

The apostle Paul shared three pictures here of what our new family, the one that we become a part of when we are reconciled to each other, looks like.

Which of these pictures do you need the most in your life right now? Why?

How would you respond to someone that says, "I love Jesus, but I don't love his church"?

Being reconciled with God doesn't mean working in unity with people is easy. Even though it's not easy to live in unity with other believers, Jesus died to bring us together. So unity must be important!

He died for His church—that's all of us—you, me, people who are different from us, and even people who are legitimately difficult to get along with!

What relationship is strained or broken in your life—especially a relationship with another Christian?

Share that with the person on your left. (You may use initials or describe the situation if you're not comfortable sharing a person's name.)

Here are a few action steps you could take this week:

1. Pray for that person.

2. Ask God to soften your heart toward him or her.

3. Call him or her.

4. Write this person a note, an email, or a text.

5. Have a face-to-face meeting.

Conclude the session with the prayer activity on the following page.

Pray

A step of faith in the right direction is worth celebrating. Whatever your step is, whether big or small, be courageous and take it this week.

Consider the following three things:

1. The grace God has shown to you through Christ.

2. The grace He has made available to all people.

3. The broken relationship you identified as being difficult to maintain unity in through your own efforts.

Take a few moments to reflect silently on Ephesians 2:13-14.

> *But now in Christ Jesus you who once were far off have been brought near by the blood of Christ. For he himself is our peace, who has made us both one and has broken down in his flesh the dividing wall of hostility*
>
> *Ephesians 2:13-14*

As you close in prayer, ask students to pray aloud for the person on their right and for the person they need to pursue a relationship with.

Prayer Requests

This Week's Plan

WORSHIP

> Read your Bible. Complete the reading plan on page 56.

> Spend time with God by engaging with the devotional experience on page 57.

> Connect with God every day in prayer.

PERSONAL STUDY

> Read and interact with "Are Small Groups Really That Important?" on page 58.

> Read and interact with "Diversity Is Essential" on page 62.

APPLICATION

> Identify an area of your life that needs to change as a result of the truth you learned in this lesson.

> Memorize Ephesians 2:13: "But now in Christ Jesus you who once were far off have been brought near by the blood of Christ."

> Connect with someone in your group this week to talk more about your thoughts on this week's study and your expectations for the group going forward.

> Continue your journal. This week, write out the many ways God has been patient and kind with you. Make a list of people that haven't earned, but most definitely need, your grace and love.

Read

Read through the following Scripture this week. Use the space provided to jot down your thoughts and responses.

Day 1: Ephesians 1

Day 2: Ephesians 2

Day 3: Ephesians 3

Day 4: Ephesians 4

Day 5: Ephesians 5

Day 6: Ephesians 6

Day 7: Ephesians 4

Reflect

ANSWERING WITH OUR ACTIONS

Did you know that one of the most beautiful marks of faith is loving other people? It is! Jesus said this:

> *"By this all people will know that you are my disciples, if you have love for one another."*
>
> *John 13:35*

How do people know that we are Christians?

How do we know that we are Christians?

The answer to this question is not simply found in thinking about something. It's found in doing. Loving other people is evidence to a lost world that we are followers of Christ.

Jesus summed up the Christian life by the way we love.

> *"Love the Lord your God with all your heart and with all your soul and with all your mind. This is the great and first commandment. And a second is like it: You shall love your neighbor as yourself. On these two commandments depend all the Law and the Prophets."*
>
> *Matthew 22:37-40*

If you want to prove to the world that you are a follower of Jesus, and prove to your heart that you truly are, love people. Don't just love people who love you back. Love those who will never love you back.

Personal study 1

ARE SMALL GROUPS REALLY THAT IMPORTANT?

You may have asked yourself this question. In fact, you may be asking yourself this question right now, three weeks into this study. Is it really worth the effort to engage in others' lives?

The Early Church

Let's start out looking at the New Testament church as it was in its beginning stages. The Book of Acts is the story of the birth, and rapid growth, of the church. Acts 2 is a key chapter that gives us a picture of the church operating in two main delivery systems: the temple courts and from house to house.

In Acts 2:14-41, Peter publicly preached the first Christian sermon and 3000 people were saved in one day. Acts 2:42-47 shows the rhythm of daily life in early church.

Read Acts 2:42-47.

> *They devoted themselves to the apostles' teaching and the fellowship, to the breaking of bread and the prayers. And awe came upon every soul, and many wonders and signs were being done through the apostles. And all who believed were together and had all things in common. And they were selling their possessions and belongings and distributing the proceeds to all, as any had need. And day by day, attending the temple together and breaking bread in their homes, they received their food with glad and generous hearts, praising God and having favor with all the people. And the Lord added to their number day by day those who were being saved.*
>
> *Acts 2:42-47*

Circle the kinds of activities that the early church did together.

Which of the above activities that you listed cannot be done (effectively) in isolation?

Which one of the benefits gets you most excited in this season of your life? Why?

Living Life in Community

Let's look at another passage. Read 1 Thessalonians 5:14.

> *We urge you, brothers, admonish the idle, encourage the fainthearted, help the weak, be patient with them all.*
>
> *1 Thessalonians 5:14*

Paul was writing to the church in Thessalonica, but he's also writing to us. We are the "brothers" he mentioned.

Underline the activities Paul encourages us to do.

Describe a time when you were able to accomplish one of these activities with someone else.

None of these activities can be done alone. In fact, they can't even be done in brief passing. It's not possible to admonish the idle (in an authentic way) in a brief passing conversation. You must be in relationship with them to even know that they are idle. The same goes for someone who is fainthearted, weak, or needs patience. The command Paul gave here implies a life lived in community, not one lived in isolation.

Day by Day

Community is something we should be scared to walk away from. Did you know that if you are living your faith out in isolation, you're in danger?

Read Hebrews 3:12-13.

> *Take care, brothers, lest there be in any of you an evil, unbelieving heart, leading you to fall away from the living God. But exhort one another every day, as long as it is called "today," that none of you may be hardened by the deceitfulness of sin.*
>
> *Hebrews 3:12-13*

This is one of the scariest verses in Scripture. We need each other because sin chips little pieces of our hearts away bit by bit. Rarely are we drawn away in an instant by huge bites. There's the real chance that sin could deceive you and draw your heart away, and you'd never even know it; your heart can be hardened without you even realizing it.

We guard our hearts by exhorting one another daily.

When was the last time you intentionally encouraged someone?

When was the last time you were encouraged, beyond the superficial, "I like your haircut" statement?

This doesn't come close to the full biblical wisdom on the value of community. But it gives a brief picture of the danger of life lived in isolation, in contrast to the beauty of life lived engaged with others.

Based on what you've learned, how would you define biblical community?

Personal Study 2

DIVERSITY IS ESSENTIAL

If Jesus' death on the cross is truly designed to bring reconciliation vertically (our relationship with God) and horizontally (with all people), shouldn't our churches be the most diverse communities on the planet? We were all aliens who "have been brought near by the blood of Christ" (Eph. 2:13). This passage doesn't just refer to band members, or athletes, or art students. It doesn't just refer to Americans coming together with Americans. We were all aliens. Every race, tribe, and tongue needed to be reconciled to one another.

> *After this I looked, and behold, a great multitude that no one could number, from every nation, from all tribes and peoples and languages, standing before the throne and before the Lamb, clothed in white robes, with palm branches in their hands, and crying out with a loud voice, "Salvation belongs to our God who sits on the throne, and to the Lamb!"*
>
> *Revelation 7:9-10*

Be honest with yourself right now. On a scale from 1 to 10, how diverse is your church?

1 — 2 — 3 — 4 — 5 — 6 — 7 — 8 — 9 — 10

NO
DIVERSITY

EVERY TRIBE,
TONGUE,
AND NATION

Why did you pick the number you picked?

What would it take to increase that number?

Before we shift the blame to others, let's check our own hearts when it comes to favoritism. We all gravitate toward people we find comfortable. For some of us, it is a money thing. Whether you say it or not, you view the poor with disdain. Or you view the rich with disdain. Or the skinny. Or the overweight.

Others of us gravitate toward a certain people group. Or away from those don't look like us. Or toward people that smell like us.

What types of people, when they walk in the room, do you try to avoid? (Honesty only helps you here.)

Read James 2:8-13.

This passage gives us great insight into the danger of showing partiality. It also gives us the remedy.

What does it mean to "love your neighbor as yourself" (Mark 12:31)?

When have you struggled to live up to that definition?

Would you rather be judged with mercy? Or without mercy?

The moment we show favoritism to someone because of the color of their skin, the money in their pocket, or the shoes on their feet is the moment we break the "royal law."

You might be tempted to throw up your hands in the air and say, "Our church is so far from being diverse and healthy…there's nothing I can do!"

I believe there is plenty you can do.

Read 1 Peter 4:8-10.

> *Above all, keep loving one another earnestly, since love covers a multitude of sins. Show hospitality to one another without grumbling. As each has received a gift, use it to serve one another, as good stewards of God's varied grace.*
>
> *1 Peter 4:8-10*

There's an implied statement in the phrase "without grumbling." The implication is that you probably have good reason to grumble. After all, when you show hospitality, people are eating your food, drinking your drinks, and making a mess of your house. Showing hospitality to others is expensive, costing you precious resources, finances, time, and emotion.

When was the last time you showed hospitality to someone who couldn't show hospitality to you in return?

Jot down the names of five people from different backgrounds who you could invite into your home.

1.

2.

3.

4.

5.

You can't possibly change everything in the world. But when you are hospitable with others, especially others that are different than you, you show the world that we serve a God who loves all people.

Don't let it stop there. Invite people from different ethnic backgrounds to your church's worship service. Advocate for vulnerable people groups. Care for orphans from other people groups, care for widows. The more we do these things, the more we bring the kingdom of God to earth and the more we prepare our hearts for heaven.

4

PURSUING UNITY IN CHRIST

Unity is one of the toughest things to pursue. Because our agendas never line up exactly, someone always has to set aside his or her own desire to unite with another person or group.

For us to pursue unity together, each person needs to choose humility. It's a two-way street, contingent upon the Holy Spirit working in each of our lives. Part of Christian unity is intentionally allowing love to win instead of our personal agendas.

When we live together in unity, we function as one unit, or body. A healthy body is a unified body. Each body part contributes its specified amount, doing its specified duty, to serve the collective whole.

When our churches bicker and complain against one another, we show ourselves to be no different than our culture. But when our local churches function together in unity, we paint a picture to the world of a good God who loves His people. A unified church is a church that is attractive to a lost world.

Ephesians 4 will teach us what a healthy, unified church looks like.

start

Use the following content to start your time together.

We've just crossed the halfway mark in this study of Ephesians.

What is something new that you've learned so far? What has really challenged your faith?

As you completed your Personal Study of Week 3, what did you learn about the value of community?

How did God use last week's memory verse, Ephesians 2:13, in your life?

In Ephesians 2 we saw how God gives us new life in Christ, and then immediately following that, beginning in Ephesians 2:11, how our new identity leads us into a new community. Ephesians 4 teaches us about how we are to live in this new community called the church.

Pray for God to open your hearts and minds before you watch the video for Session 4.

watch

Use the space below to follow along and take notes as you watch video Session 4.

1. The church is a _____.

2. A healthy church is marked by spiritual _____.

3. We're united by _____, _____, and a common _____.

4. This is a _____ to be part of the body of Christ.

5. A healthy church is marked by spiritual _____.

6. If you're _____ spiritually, it's not for your benefit. It's for the benefit of the church.

7. A healthy church is marked by a growing _____.

8. What happens when you have a _____ in the church? You can fight, you can flee, or you can follow Ephesians 4.

Scripture: Ephesians 4:1-16

Answers: 1. body 2. unity 3. calling, character, confession 4. privilege 5. citizens 6. gifted 7. maturity 8. conflict

Discuss

As we continue our discussion on unity, think through the context of your local church.

What evidence have you seen that your church is characterized by a supernatural unity?

What action steps have you personally taken to fight against disunity?

Read Ephesians 4:1-3.

How would you define the characteristics that Paul used to describe the Christian life? (Humility, Gentleness, Patience, Love)

What is the opposite of each of those character qualities?

How have you seen each of these contributing to or drawing away from eagerly maintaining "the unity of the Spirit in the bond of peace"?

People don't drift toward unity, but away from it. Part of "maintaining" sometimes means having difficult conversations. God often shows up in these awkward conversations as we're trying to reconcile differences. It shouldn't surprise us because Jesus cares about the unity of His church.

When was the last time you "maintained" unity by having a difficult conversation with someone?

Knowing what you know about the value of unity for the health of your church, how would you begin a difficult conversation now?

Tony highlights the 3 main things that unite us:

1. Character (Eph. 4:2)

2. Calling (Eph. 4:4)

3. Confession (Eph. 4:4-6)

How have you seen these qualities build unity among Christians?

How have you seen damaging effects in relationships, and specifically in a church, when any of these three areas are neglected?

Tony says in the video:

Some people say, "I don't see any need for a church. I don't see how the church is going to bless me." That's wrong-headed thinking, so I flip it on them and say, "Have you ever thought that the church needs you and your spiritual gifts?"

How would you help someone who "doesn't need church" see the mutual benefit of community with a story from your own life?

How have you used your spiritual gifts in the church?

In what ways does diversity benefit the church?

Conclude the session with the prayer activity on the following page.

Pray

We talked through lots of different spiritual gifts, and how each of us is gifted to serve. Jot down a couple of different spiritual gifts God has given you.

We also talked through four character qualities required to maintain unity:

1. Humility

2. Gentleness

3. Patience

4. Love

Circle the one you need to work on the most.

Get into groups (girls with girls, guys with guys) of two or three and confess the character quality you need to work on. If you're comfortable, pray aloud for one other person in the group. Ask God to identify specific, creative, unique ways they can use their gifts to build the strength of your small group and your local church.

Prayer Requests

This Week's Plan

WORSHIP

> Read your Bible. Complete the reading plan on page 74.

> Spend time with God by engaging with the devotional experience on page 75.

> Connect with God every day in prayer.

PERSONAL STUDY

> Read and interact with "Unity or Uniformity?" on page 76.

> Read and interact with "Knowledge and Love" on page 80.

APPLICATION

> Identify an area of your life that needs to change as a result of the truth you learned in this session.

> Memorize Ephesians 4:1-3: "I therefore, a prisoner for the Lord, urge you to walk in a manner worthy of the calling to which you have been called, with all humility and gentleness, with patience, bearing with one another in love, eager to maintain the unity of the Spirit in the bond of peace."

> Connect with someone in your group this week to talk more about your thoughts on this week's study and your expectations for the group going forward.

> Continue your journal. This week, write out some ways you could work to live in harmony with others in your local church. Think through some ways you can do this well and some ways you have messed up.

Read

Read through the following Scripture this week. Use the space provided to jot down your thoughts and responses.

Day 1: Ephesians 1

Day 2: Ephesians 2

Day 3: Ephesians 3

Day 4: Ephesians 4

Day 5: Ephesians 5

Day 6: Ephesians 6

Day 7: Ephesians 4:27-32; 5:1-17

Reflect

You Get a Superpower, and You Get a Superpower, and You Get a Superpower!

You know you have superpowers, right? You, yes you, have been given a spiritual gift, a supernatural power. Check out 1 Corinthians 12:7-10; Romans 12:6-8; and Ephesians 4:11 to get an idea of some of the gifts God has given us. Did you realize, though, that the spiritual gifts you've been given are not really for you? First Peter 4:10 says, "As each has received a gift, use it to serve one another, as good stewards of God's varied grace."

First Corinthians 12:7 says, "To each is given the manifestation of the Spirit for the common good."

Our gifts collectively make up the body of Christ. This means that if you don't exercise your spiritual gift, not only do you lose out on the joy of expressing your God-given gift, we all lose out because our body isn't complete. There are two truths we can notice about our gifts from this passage:

> Our spiritual gifts are a manifestation of the Spirit. So without you exercising your gifts, the Holy Spirit is not made present through you to others. That's a lot of responsibility!

> Your spiritual gift is designed "for the common good," which means that without you exercising the Holy Spirit, our "good" is not as "good" as it could be.

Which of the above truths, these major responsibilities, resonates most deeply with you? Why?

This week, as you reflect on the spiritual gifts God has given you, reflect on how you can use those gifts to bless and serve others.

Personal Study 1

Unity or Uniformity?

As we have dug in to the concept of unity, you may be tempted to equate unity with uniformity. These are different concepts. Unity means we are working at peace, together with one another. Uniformity means we are working to become the same person, clones of one another as we lose our unique identity.

How are we called to pursue unity, and not uniformity? There are three primary ways.

In Our Gifting

Our giftings are unique. They're a supernatural gift from God given to us to serve others. They're influenced by our past hurts and failures, our successes, our parents and our influences. They're shaped by where we live and the environments God has allowed us to walk through. They're molded by our personality.

They're unique to you. I see the value of the gift of administration, but I sure don't have it! If I force you to look just like me and have my gifts, we become a church with a huge arm but no legs. Or we become a church with a massive nose but no chin. *Eww.*

We tend to look at others' gifts, though, and wish they were ours. You wish you were better at teaching than her. You wish you were better at hospitality, like he is. But we forget that if we don't express our gifts, our whole church loses.

Read 1 Corinthians 12:22-24.

> *On the contrary, the parts of the body that seem to be weaker are indispensable, and on those parts of the body that we think less honorable we bestow the greater honor, and our unpresentable parts are treated with greater modesty, which our more presentable parts do not require. But God has so composed the body, giving greater honor to the part that lacked it.*
>
> *1 Corinthians 12:22-24*

In our human economy we think the most important gifts are the ones that are seen publicly. But Paul points out that the "parts of the body that we think less honorable we bestow the greater honor…" (v. 23). He flips our scale on its head.

How have you used your spiritual gifts to serve others in the last month?

Do you have spiritual gifts that are noticed? Based on 1 Corinthians 12:22-24, why is this significant?

When you try to conform your gifts to match someone else's, we all lose. Your gifts go unexpressed, and our body of believers becomes weaker. Live in unity, not uniformity.

Over the Nonessentials

Read 1 Corinthians 3:3-9.

The question is not whether you have problems in your church. The question is how you can contribute to the unity of the church. We don't contribute to unity by fighting with one another. In the passage above, we're told that we're acting in the flesh when we are jealous or full of strife.

It's easy to disagree with someone and dismiss them because of their beliefs. That's what was going on in the Corinthian church. Individuals were uniting themselves with the teachings of different leaders and disagreeing with anyone who thought differently.

It's not wrong to disagree with someone, especially over secondary issues.

Remembering which issues are primary and which are secondary is important when it comes to unity. (See Ephesians 4:4-6 for the primary theological ideas.) But it's not healthy to divide over secondary issues, and claim allegiance to a certain teacher over allegiance to God.

What kinds of issues are secondary? (Secondary issues are any that the Bible has not spoken clearly on.)

Over what issues have you seen relationships broken that the Bible hasn't spoken clearly on?

Describe a time in your life when someone set aside preferences for the sake of loving you.

Uniformity says, "We all have to believe the exact same thing about every single Scripture in order to have fellowship together." Unity says, "I love you enough to disagree, but maintain fellowship."

What happens when people make secondary issues of primary importance?

When We're Sinned Against

What should we do when we're sinned against? Uniformity would say, "We just all need to agree, even when one person was hurt." Unity says, "Our relationship is broken, and I love you enough to work to restore what we lost."

Read Matthew 18:15-20.

When have you restored unity in the way that Jesus taught in this passage?

The opposite of the Matthew 18 approach would be to gossip about a person instead of going to him or her directly.

When have you seen gossip break down unity? What should we do to stop gossip?

So, the question is are you going to let your secondary issue agenda win? Or are you going to put on the virtues of Christ, maintain unity, and have the difficult conversations necessary for the good of the church and the glory of God?

Personal study 2

Knowledge and Love

In Ephesians 4:14, we learn that we should no longer be:

> … *children, tossed to and fro by the waves and carried about by every wind of doctrine, by human cunning, by craftiness in evil schemes.*
>
> *Ephesians 4:14*

As we grow up in our faith, it's so important that we grow in our understanding of sound, biblical doctrine. Otherwise, as Paul said here, we're prone to being tossed around with every doctrine and theological fad that comes along.

But there's a proper and improper application of this verse. Let's look at another time that Paul wrote about being a child.

Read 1 Corinthians chapter 13 and then pay special attention to verse 11 below.

> *When I was a child, I spoke like a child, I thought like a child, I reasoned like a child. When I became a man, I gave up childish ways.*
>
> *1 Corinthians 13:11*

Imagine a two-year-old kid. She speaks, thinks, and reasons like a child. If you could sum all of that up in one phrase, it would be this: "It's all about me!" Everything she does is about meeting her own desires. And if you get in the way of her pursuit, she'll let you know.

In 1 Corinthians 13, Paul equated maturity with love. To "give up childish ways" means to pursue love, not just our own self-interest. As important as it is to learn sound doctrine, we should never sacrifice the application of that doctrine. It's the difference between head knowledge and heart knowledge.

Think of people you know who have been consumed by their pursuit of knowledge. How did being around them make you feel?

Babies are cute. We love to hold them, hear them make little baby noises, give them bottles, and watch them roll around. But those same noises, behaviors, and actions aren't so cute as a baby turns into an adult. If you were to walk into someone's home and the dad was cooing in his crib while looking up at a spinning mobile, you'd be right to think that something was wrong.

In a similar way, when you become a Christian, you are a baby. And that's good! Babies do baby things. But you aren't to stay that way. You need to learn and grow.

What are some of the most important doctrines new believers should wrap their heads and hearts around?

What are some of the most important behaviors a maturing believer should practice?

In what ways are you prone to show an immature faith?

> *If I…understand all mysteries and all knowledge, …but have not love, I am nothing.*
>
> *1 Corinthians 13:2*

Can you imagine if you could understand all mysteries and all knowledge? How powerful would you be? How historic would you be? How…unbearable would you be? You'd never be wrong! Love may not give us power or write our names in history books, but it gives us and others value. Love is the proper application of knowledge.

Be honest. Can you remember a time when you erred on the "I'm right and you're wrong" side of an argument?

In that situation how could you have let love win?

In another passage in 1 Corinthians, Paul said, "'knowledge' puffs up, but love builds up" (1 Cor. 8:1). Knowledge can make you look good and feel good. Have you ever heard the phrase, "He's got a big head!"? People get a "big head" because they increase in knowledge (usually about themselves), but don't increase in love.

As we begin following Christ, our knowledge about ourselves increases greatly! The Bible even calls us "saints." Knowledge alone builds us up, but it's not guaranteed to build others up (at least not in and of itself). It may build you up, but that's where it stops. However, love makes the whole body stronger.

What knowledge have you gained so far in this study?

List a few practical ways that love can flow out of your knowledge.

As we're looking to live out Ephesians 4:14, not being tossed around by every wind and doctrine, let's not forget Ephesians 4:15, living out truth and love:

Rather, speaking the truth in love, we are to grow up in every way into him who is the head, into Christ.

Ephesians 4:15

SESSION

5

PURSUING HOLINESS IN CHRIST

Do you ever hear the ice cream truck blaring its horn through your neighborhood? It brings back childhood memories of standing in the road staring at the side of the ice cream truck trying to decide between an ice cream sandwich, or a chocolate/vanilla combo served in the shape of a cartoon character with a cold, stale piece of bubble gum waiting for you at the end. Ahh, nostalgia.

As children, ice cream trucks seemed almost magical. The older you become, though, the more the distorted horn sounds like the music from a horror movie. It makes you wonder why you ever thought buying ice cream out of the busted window of a stranger's rusty van was okay.

As we grow up, our perspectives change. We start to see a bigger picture that isn't focused on what we think we want in any given moment. Sometimes, though, we slip back into "childish" ways, reaching for ice cream out of a rusty van.

We should all hope that, as time progresses, we find ourselves growing closer to the Lord. Our walk with Christ should continue to become more intimate (progressive sanctification) as we seek to put off our old self, our former way of life, and put on our new self which has been created to be like God, full of holiness (Eph. 4:22-24).

This week we're going to take a look at holiness and its practical implications in our lives.

start

Use the following content to start your time together.

Last week, we talked about spiritual gifts and how we each have been gifted to serve and build up the body of Christ—the Church. Without each of us expressing our supernatural gifts, we suffer individually and corporately.

What did you learn about the difference between unity and uniformity?

How did you apply the truths from the personal study, "Knowledge and Love" (pp. 80-83) in the following areas of your life?

Home

Work

School

With your neighbors

This week we will be talking through holiness and its implications for our daily lives. How do we pursue holiness? What should we do when we mess up? What kinds of behaviors and attitudes should mark God's people who are pursuing holiness?

Pray for God to open your hearts and minds before you watch the video for Session 5.

watch

Use the space below to follow along and take notes as you watch video Session 5.

1. Positionally, we're _____. We are _____. We've been declared righteous. This is all because of the work of Christ.

2. _____ and holiness are not at odds. They go together.

3. God's _____ for our lives involves the pursuit of holiness.

4. Walk in _____, _____, and _____.

5. Love involves compassion that leads to _____.

6. The Christian is not just to _____ darkness. We are to _____ darkness as well.

7. We walk in wisdom by being filled with the _____.

Scripture: Ephesians 4:17–5:17

Answers: 1. saints, holy 2. Happiness 3. will 4. love, light, wisdom 5. action 6. avoid, expose 7. Spirit

Discuss

In the video, Tony mentioned two types of holiness that we should keep in mind any time we're reading a passage in the Bible about holiness.

> **What are they? Which of the two types does Ephesians 4–5 address?**
>
> **Which of the two types should define your identity? Why?**

When it comes to holiness, our culture often thinks of a caricatured holier-than-thou type of person. But Scripture paints a different picture.

> **What are some common misconceptions when it comes to a cultural understanding of "holiness"?**

Some people believe we find holiness when we isolate ourselves from others and from the world.

> **Why is isolationism not holiness? How did Jesus demonstrate perfect holiness, even while interacting with sinners?**

> **Tony says, "The reason there's so little happiness in our world today is there's so little holiness in our world today." What did he mean? Do you believe that? Why or why not?**

Our culture confuses love with four ideas: lust, tolerance, everything, a feeling.

> **Why is each of these not true, Christ-honoring love?**

So, how do we love? We love as Christ loved us and gave Himself for us. Love involves compassion that leads to action.

Read Ephesians 5:2.

Using this Scripture as your guide, give a biblical definition of love.

When you think of the word "love," be honest—what do you tend to think? Have you ever loved someone with a biblical kind of love?

Read Ephesians 4:19-32 aloud together as a small group. As you read, make note of the sins that Paul listed.

Pursuing holiness is about identifying the sinful behaviors and attitudes so you can apply the "put off/put on" principle. You can read more about this in the Personal Study titled "The Put Off/Put On Principle" this week. As God exposes certain sins in your life, you have the opportunity to put that sin off, and in its place put on a character trait that honors God.

What sins, as you look through this text, do you need to repent of?

Tony shared that in our pursuit of holiness, the three ways we're to walk are: in love, in the light, and in wisdom.

What does it mean for you to live a holy life in each of the previous three areas (love, light, and wisdom):

at school?

in your neighborhood?

on your team?

Conclude the session with the prayer activity on the following page.

Pray

Maybe this week exposed some areas in our lives that we need to work on. Thankfully, as we learned in Week 3, we don't have to work alone! In fact, it would be foolish of us to think we could fight against our weaknesses by ourselves.

By this time your group should be comfortable enough with one another to confess an area where you're weak. Break up into smaller groups by gender. Guys with guys. Girls with girls.

Read James 5:16 aloud together as a group.

> *Confess your sins to one another and pray for one another, that you may be healed. The prayer of a righteous person has great power as it is working.*
>
> James 5:16

Ask if people are willing to share weaknesses they're facing right now, in light of the passage we read this week.

As you share requests and close in prayer, ask the Holy Spirit to give you success this week in the areas where sin is creeping in. Be sure to follow up with one another throughout the week.

Prayer Requests

Encourage people to complete "This Week's Plan" before the next group session.

This Week's Plan

WORSHIP

〉 Read your Bible. Complete the reading plan on page 92.

〉 Spend time with God by engaging with the devotional experience on page 93.

〉 Connect with God every day in prayer.

PERSONAL STUDY

〉 Read and interact with "Living in the Light" on page 94.

〉 Read and interact with "The Put Off/Put On Principle" on page 98.

APPLICATION

〉 Identify an area of your life that needs to change as a result of the truth you learned in this lesson.

〉 Memorize Ephesians 5:2: "Walk in love, as Christ loved us and gave himself up for us, a fragrant offering and sacrifice to God."

〉 Connect with someone in your group this week to talk more about your thoughts on this week's study and your expectations for the group going forward.

〉 Continue your journal. This week record your thoughts on your identity, especially in light of all of the truth we've uncovered in this study.

Read

Read through the following Scripture this week. Use the space provided to jot down your thoughts and responses.

Day 1: Ephesians 1

Day 2: Ephesians 2

Day 3: Ephesians 3

Day 4: Ephesians 4

Day 5: Ephesians 5

Day 6: Ephesians 6

Day 7: Reread Ephesians 6, focusing on verses 1-10.

Reflect

DIFFERENT FROM THE WORLD

If you don't look any different than the world, are you really pursuing holiness?

How do you look different from the world in the way you—spend your money? Fill your days? Fill up your free time? Talk to your parents? Give generously of your resources? Find contentment?

Psalm 24:3-4 says:

> *Who shall ascend the hill of the LORD?*
> *And who shall stand in his holy place?*
> *He who has clean hands and a pure heart,*
> *who does not lift up his soul to what is false*
> *and does not swear deceitfully.*
>
> *Psalm 24:3-4*

In our practical holiness, we should be set apart from the world. This isn't a detachment, where we live life in isolation so we can avoid all influences from culture. This is intentionally living in such a way that others "may see your good deeds and glorify God on the day he visits us" (1 Pet. 2:12, NIV).

Can you imagine that? What if someone who was completely lost, apart from Christ, saw the way you lived? Would he or she be impressed by your love, mercy, generosity, and contentment? Or would they say, "We're just the same"? It's our passionate pursuit of Christ that causes our lives to look different than (though not detached from) the world.

If you weren't able to speak, would others know you follow Jesus?

Personal Study 1

LIVING IN THE LIGHT

We learned in this week's study that one of the ways we are to walk as followers of Jesus (who are pursuing holiness) is "in the light."

Let's dive a little deeper and see what this means.

Read 1 John 1:7.

> *If we walk in the light, as he is in the light, we have fellowship with one another, and the blood of Jesus his Son cleanses us from all sin.*
>
> *1 John 1:7*

In the broader context of this passage (1 John 1:5-10), we see light contrasted with darkness. God is light. Sin is darkness. The ways of God are light. The ways of our flesh are darkness. Then we get to verse 7, which doesn't just tell us to dabble our toe in the light. It doesn't just tell us to practice in the light or look at the light. We're commanded to "walk" in the light. Walking is an everyday activity, one that's always moving us forward. The cost of discipleship is that we don't simply turn our backs on our former lives and stay put. We are called to "walk" the other way in the light.

As we do this, "we have fellowship with one another." Fellowship is more than just a potluck at church or pizza with your small group. Paul took "fellowship" to another level when he compared our relationship with others and our "walking in the light." He did this because we can't have true fellowship with one another until we have true fellowship with Jesus. Because our fellowship is rooted in our identity: We're unworthy followers of the King in need of daily grace.

How have you seen "walking in the light" affect fellowship?

How have you seen "walking in the darkness" affect fellowship?

Read Ephesians 5:8-9,13.

> *for at one time you were darkness, but now you are light in the Lord. Walk as children of light (for the fruit of light is found in all that is good and right and true)…but when anything is exposed by the light, it becomes visible.*
>
> *Ephesians 5:8-9,13*

In verse 8, Paul said, "At one time you were darkness." Notice it's not that you "were walking in darkness" (though that's true). It is "you were darkness." Now, he says, "you are light in the Lord." So, your identity has changed. If your identity has changed, your behaviors and attitudes should change, too.

As followers of Christ, we know we're not supposed to live in darkness. We're commanded not to pursue sin. But Paul takes this a step further. He calls us to not just avoid darkness, but to expose it as well. We have an obligation to avoid and expose. It's like we're standing in a dark room with a flashlight screaming to everyone else who will hear: "Stay away from that!"

"See it? There it is! Get away! It's dangerous!" That's the message we use as we shine our light into the darkness.

In what areas of our culture does darkness seem to prevail?

What can you and your small group, or even you and your local church, do to expose the darkness?

Before you get too overwhelmed by the darkness, and the way our culture around the world seems to be consumed by it, let's grab some hope.

Read John 1:1-5.

Verse 5 says this:

> *The light shines in the darkness, and the darkness has not overcome it.*
>
> *John 1:5*

When light shows up, darkness goes away. Don't believe me? Try standing in a dark room and turning on a light. Doesn't the darkness scatter? Doesn't it run? After 60 seconds, does the darkness start encroaching back on its lost territory? No! The light continues to win!

Do you know who "the light" refers to in John 1:5? It's Jesus Himself. And He's already defeated death and darkness. Our King has won the battle, and we get to share in His spoils. We get to walk in the light!

Our Light, Jesus, said these words:

> *"You are the light of the world. A city set on a hill cannot be hidden. Nor do people light a lamp and put it under a basket, but on a stand, and it gives light to all in the house. In the same way, let your light shine before others, so that they may see your good works and give glory to your Father who is in heaven."*
>
> *Matthew 5:14-16*

We, the church, are the light of the world. And our light cannot be hidden unless we actively choose to try to hide it. And when our light comes in to a place, it "gives light to all in the house" (Matt. 5:15).

Don't be overwhelmed by the darkness. Rather, fight against the darkness with the one thing that has the power to overcome it: light.

Personal study 2

THE PUT OFF/PUT ON PRINCIPLE

In Ephesians 4 and 5, we see Paul urging us to "put off" lots of different activities. Read Ephesians 4:25–5:11 again.

In this passage, Paul commanded us to "put off" things like: lying, anger, stealing, corrupt talk, bitterness, slander, malice, filthiness, foolish talk, and crude joking.

We can work to stop doing these things. We can try to "put them off." But the problem is that these are behaviors driven by our hearts. They're not simply actions existing in a bubble. They're driven by our motives and desires. So to stop the action without replacing it with an action that reorients our heart toward Jesus will cause a vacuum to form. When the vacuum forms within our heart, some other behavior rushes in its place.

Have you ever heard of a "dry drunk"? This is someone that was formerly addicted to alcohol. They're not anymore, so they're technically considered "dry." Those that know them best will tell you that they haven't had a drop of alcohol but have substituted another issue in its place. They don't drink, but they've got a short fuse. They don't drink, but they deal with anger issues. They don't drink, but they are full of resentment.

They've simply replaced one behavior with another, never addressing the root cause of their addiction: a heart that's bent on something other than God. So when one sinful behavior is removed, and no God-honoring activity is put in its place, the heart remains unchanged.

So Paul said, for each of the sins above, to put off/put on:

> Lying $\longrightarrow$ speaking the truth

> Anger $\longrightarrow$ active reconciliation

> Stealing $\longrightarrow$ doing honest work

> Corrupt talk $\longrightarrow$ build others up

> Bitterness ➝ kindness

> Slander ➝ tenderheartedness

> Malice ➝ forgiveness

> Filthiness ➝ thanksgiving

> Foolish talk ➝ thanksgiving

> Crude joking ➝ thanksgiving

Have you ever known people who changed their behaviors, but their hearts remained the same? What action step should those people have substituted for the behaviors they were trying to change?

Ephesians 5:15 tells us:

Look carefully then how you walk, not as unwise but as wise.

Ephesians 5:15

There are some behaviors that we simply need to replace with God-honoring ones. There are other behaviors, addictions in particular, that we need to be even more aggressive with. Instead of simply replacing the sinful habit with a God-honoring one, we may need to remove ourselves from the environment completely. "Look carefully… how you walk" (Eph. 5:15). Be diligent with every step, and pursue wisdom. If Paul were writing to you today, maybe he'd say something like, "You need to 'put off' that job." Or, "You need to 'put off' that relationship." Or maybe Paul would say, "You need to 'put off' that whole city. Get out of there. It's too strong of a pull on your heart."

Is there an area of your life you need to start looking at more carefully?

Who would you like to surround yourself with who can help you live "not as unwise but as wise"? Record their name(s) below.

Why is this so important?

Read Romans 13:11.

> *Besides this you know the time, that the hour has come for you to wake from sleep. For salvation is nearer to us now than when we first believed.*
>
> *Romans 13:11*

Friends, it's time to wake up. If we have behaviors in our lives that need to change, let's get creative. Let's find ways to fight against our sin. "The hour has come" for us to "wake from sleep." No more slumbering! If there are behaviors that need to be "put off," let's do the hard work of cleansing our lives of those activities that are dragging us down. Let's find the equal, yet opposite, behavior that through the power of the Holy Spirit will work to change our hearts.

This verse serves as a reminder to us that none of us know the hour when Jesus will come. But we can say with great confidence that we are closer to His second coming today than we were yesterday. So let's buckle down.

What do you think your best friend would say if you asked what areas of your spiritual life you need to work on?

How would you suggest "putting on" the equal yet opposite behavior?

As we continue through this study, may we regularly pray with the psalmist:

Create in me a clean heart, O God,
and renew a right spirit within me.

Psalm 51:10

SESSION

6

BE STRONG IN CHRIST

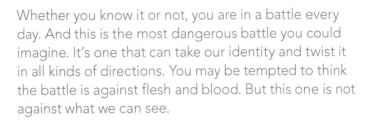

Whether you know it or not, you are in a battle every day. And this is the most dangerous battle you could imagine. It's one that can take our identity and twist it in all kinds of directions. You may be tempted to think the battle is against flesh and blood. But this one is not against what we can see.

Weapons of the flesh aren't going to work against this Enemy. We've got to be equipped with armor of a different kind if we're going to be ready for the Enemy that's coming our way.

Like a warrior in an army, we don't have to head to the battlefield unprotected. Thankfully, we're not left to fight on our own or forge our own battle gear. God has provided armor for us. We're going to need to utilize every piece of what God gives us to protect every part of ourselves. Even though (spoiler alert!) the ultimate battle is already won!

This week's final session will help equip you for daily continuing to fight for your identity as unseen forces all around you fight to rob and destroy you.

start

Use the following content to start your time together.

We've made it to the final week! Last week, we studied the biblical concept of holiness. We saw that the Bible teaches a holiness that looks different than what the world thinks holiness is. We also saw that true, Christ-honoring love is action-oriented. It's not simply a lust or a feeling.

As you read "Living in the Light" (pp. 94-97) in your Personal Study, did you identify any areas you personally would like to have "exposed by the light" (Eph. 5:13)?

How could your group get involved in this process with you?

In our final week of study, Tony walks through part of the final chapter of Ephesians, as we look together at the armor God provides for us to fight against unseen forces that wage a war against us. There is an all-out war against our holiness and against our identity. It's time to suit up.

Pray for God to open your hearts and minds before you watch the video for Session 6.

watch

Use the space below to follow along and take notes as you watch video Session 6.

1. We're made for _____.

2. There's an _____ element to this battle.

3. There's a _____ element.

4. There's an _____ element.

5. There's a _____ element.

6. Our _____ is in our union with Christ. It's in our identity in Christ.

7. Don't go into the battle without a _____. Don't go into the battle without a sword.

8. The first step to fighting spiritual warfare is to really _____ a battle's going on.

Scripture: Ephesians 6:10-20

Answers: 1. battle 2. internal 3. defensive 4.offensiv 5. corporate 6. strength 7. weapon 8. believe

Discuss

In this week's video Tony introduced the armor of God we need to fight the spiritual powers that work against us.

Were you ever in a physical fight as a kid? How did things turn out?

We may be tempted to think that Satan is just found in things like terrorist attacks. But in reality, Satan would love nothing more than to destroy the everyday relationships you have in your local church and within your family.

Read Ephesians 6:10.

Based on what you've learned so far in this study, brainstorm with your group some ways you can "be strong in the Lord."

What habits did you start during this study that you plan to continue in the future?

Read Ephesians 6:11-13.

We don't fight this battle using our own strength, our own resources, or our own abilities. The strength mentioned in verses 10-13 implies that the Devil can truly be defeated. That's great news!

On a scale of 1 to 10 (1 being not at all, 10 being fully ready), how equipped do you feel to do daily battle against Satan?

1 —— 2 —— 3 —— 4 —— 5 —— 6 —— 7 —— 8 —— 9 —— 10

NOT AT ALL   FULL READY

What would help increase this number?

Read through Ephesians 6:14-17.

Paul mentioned the following equipment in this passage:

The belt of truth (v. 14)

The breastplate of righteousness (v. 14)

Gospel shoes (v. 15)

Shield of faith (v. 16)

Helmet of salvation (v. 17)

Sword of the Spirit (v. 17)

Which pieces are defensive? Explain the value and meaning of each.

What is the only offensive weapon? Why is this important?

In relation to the pieces of armor, what area of your life is most vulnerable?

In the video Tony says, "If you're not in the battle, by daily Bible reading, meditation, and using your Bible reading as a catalyst for your prayers, then start."

What does your Bible-reading plan look like? How are you disciplining yourself in this area?

How has the weekly reading plan been helpful for you?

What difference have you noticed in your life when you spend consistent time in Scripture?

Close your time together with the prayer activity on the following page.

Pray

Hopefully you don't find yourself in a physical battle this week, but spiritual battles are going on all around us all of the time. Satan and his army would love to wreck our identities, our jobs, our churches, our families, and our communities.

Spend some time now sharing ways you feel that any one of these areas is under attack in your life right now.

As you close your time together, pray specifically for anyone who shared a difficulty. Don't pray generic prayers, but specific ones. Pray for each other by name and for each situation in detail. When we pray specifically, God can answer specifically, and we know precisely how to thank Him when He comes through for us!

Ask the Holy Spirit to guide each of you as you continue living life battle-ready.

Prayer Requests

Encourage people to complete "This Week's Plan" on their own. Begin the conversation now, if your group hasn't already, about what you're going to study next. You can find a list of suggested resources at *lifeway.com.*

This Week's Plan

WORSHIP

> Continue to read your Bible daily. Start by reading Paul's next letter, Philippians.

> Spend time with God by engaging with the devotional experience on page 110.

> Connect with God every day in prayer.

PERSONAL STUDY

> Read and interact with "Obedience-Shaped Relationships" on page 112.

> Read and interact with "Should I Stay, or Should I Go?" on page 116.

APPLICATION

> Identify an area of your life that needs to change as a result of the truth you learned in this lesson.

> Memorize Ephesians 6:10-11: "Finally, be strong in the Lord and in the strength of his might. Put on the whole armor of God, that you may be able to stand against the schemes of the devil."

> Connect with someone in your group this week to talk more about your thoughts on this week's study and your expectations for the group going forward.

> Continue your journal. This week, record ways you see Satan working against you, trying to undermine the identity you have in Christ.

Read

Day 1: Ephesians 1

Day 2: Ephesians 2

Day 3: Ephesians 3

Day 4: Ephesians 4

Day 5: Ephesians 5

Day 6: Ephesians 6

Day 7: Philippians 1

Reflect

I'LL TELL MY DAD!

As an elementary-school student, the phrase "I'll tell my dad!" was the ultimate trump card. It would end every single argument, fuss, and squabble.

When it comes to the battles we face every day (like the ones Paul mentioned in Ephesians 6), we need backup. This isn't a battle we can fight with our own strength, our own weapons, or even our own reputation. We can truly do nothing apart from Christ. Read Jesus' words:

> *I am the vine; you are the branches. Whoever abides in me and I in him, he it is that bears much fruit, for apart from me you can do nothing.*
>
> *John 15:5*

What challenges has God placed in front of you that you need to face by "abiding" in Him?

The next time Satan tempts you, speak these words to him: "I'll tell my Dad!" God will have your back, every single time. He will never leave you alone. He'll never leave you exposed in battle. And the moment you call on Him is the moment you'll realize He's right beside you.

> *Fear not, for I am with you;*
> *be not dismayed, for I am your God;*
> *I will strengthen you, I will help you,*
> *I will uphold you with my righteous right hand.*
>
> *Isaiah 41:10*

What area of your life right now is marked by fear?

How can you apply the truth of God's presence to your fear?

Personal Study 1

OBEDIENCE-SHAPED RELATIONSHIPS
Command: Obey Your Parents

Children don't have to be taught disobedience. Disobedience comes naturally, but we have to be taught to do what's right. We have to be taught the gospel.

Read Ephesians 6:1.

> *Children, obey your parents in the Lord, for this is right.*
>
> *Ephesians 6:1*

How is being obedient to your parents related to the gospel? (*Hint: Check out Ex. 20:12; John 14:15; and 1 John 3:24*).

How did your parents, or other mature Christians, help you understand the gospel?

Read Deuteronomy 6:5-9.

> *You shall love the LORD your God with all your heart and with all your soul and with all your might. And these words that I command you today shall be on your heart. You shall teach them diligently to your children, and shall talk of them when you sit in your house, and when you walk by the way, and when you lie down, and when you rise. You shall bind them as a sign on your hand, and they shall be as frontlets between your eyes. You shall write them on the doorposts of your house and on your gates.*
>
> *Deuteronomy 6:5-9*

We're called to love God with all of our heart, soul, and might. The passage says you should talk of these things "when you sit in your house, and when you walk by the way, and when you lie down and when you rise" (v. 7). Although you may not have kids yet, it's important to learn about the gospel within our families.

Look at the ways we're supposed to learn about God's commands within our families:

› When you sit in your house

› When you walk by the way

› When you lie down

› When you rise

Notice: Your Obedience Reflects Your Relationship with the Lord

Read John 14:15-17.

> *If you love me, you will keep my commandments. And I will ask the Father, and he will give you another Helper, to be with you forever, even the Spirit of truth, whom the world cannot receive, because it neither sees him nor knows him. You know him, for he dwells with you and will be in you.*
>
> *John 14:15-17*

According to verse 15, why do we keep God's commands?

Highlight the word "Helper" in verse 16. Where does this Helper go with you? How long will this Helper be with you?

How is obedience to God's commands possible? How does it help you to know that the Holy Spirit helps you to live in obedience to God?

Read 1 John 3:24.

> *Whoever keeps his commandments abides in God, and God in him. And by this we know that he abides in us, by the Spirit whom he has given us.*
>
> *1 John 3:24*

How does this verse tie in to the truth we read in John 14:15-17?

In what way does this verse further your understanding of the importance of obedience in the Christian life?

Reward: A Promise of Life

So often we're reminded of the Ten Commandments, the importance of obeying and honoring our parents, and how our obedience to them reflects our relationship with the Lord.

Even if your parents are not believers, they are in a God-appointed role of authority in your life. They are not perfect, but they do have wisdom and experience (including mistakes) that you can learn from. You are still to honor them.

Read Ephesians 6:2-3.

> *"Honor your father and mother" (this is the first commandment with a promise), "that it may go well with you and that you may live long in the land."*
>
> *Ephesians 6:2-3*

Think about this: As a child, you are a recipient of the first command to include a promise. God gives promises throughout the Bible, but none so specific to your relationship with your parents.

What does this promise mean to you, personally?

List two steps to help you honor and obey your parents, even when it's difficult.

Personal Study 2

SHOULD I STAY, OR SHOULD I GO?

When temptations comes our way, should we stand and fight? Or turn and run? Do we stand strong like a soldier? Or run away? Do we fight? Or does God do the fighting for us? Do we suit up with armor or rest in our identity?

The answer is: "It depends." There are three different scenarios we will take a look at, with three very different responses that Scripture calls us to.

God Will Fight for Us

Read at least one of the following passages: Exodus 14:14; 2 Chronicles 20:17; or Deuteronomy 3:22.

To trust that God will fight our battles for us means to trust that—even when our lives seem hopeless and we feel overwhelmed, in the moments and seasons when we're tempted to doubt God's presence and doubt that He even cares— God fights our battles for us. He will supply all of our needs according to His riches (Phil. 4:19). He makes good plans for us, even when those plans won't come to fruition for years (Jer. 29:11). And His ways are higher than ours (Isa. 55:8-9).

We ask God to fight for us when we're discouraged or afraid.

When have you needed the reminder that God fights your battles?

What situations in life bring you great discouragement?

Describe a time in your life when you were afraid of what was coming.

How can you use the truth of these passages to conquer your fear?

Stand and Fight

Read at least one of the following passages, highlighting the action verbs: 1 Peter 5:8-9; Ephesians 6:11-14; or James 1:12.

We're called to stand and fight Satan. Standing and fighting is different than "asking God to fight for us." We are called to stand and fight when we're under trial. It's when we're suffering that we should fight. Satan is prowling around like a lion ready to devour us, but if we stand firm (knowing it's by the strength of God we stand, not our own), we will win. Daily, sometimes hourly, we're called to fight. It's through suffering that God forms us into the image of Jesus (Rom. 8:28-29) and creates a ministry for us by which we can serve others (2 Cor. 1:4-7).

When have you stood your ground and fought Satan?

Has there been a cause for which you've stood up and fought? Did you feel like Satan was working against you?

How does the truth that others are suffering around the world (1 Pet. 5:9) embolden your faith and your fight?

Turn and Flee

We're called to turn and flee temptations when they come our way. Especially sexual sins.

Read the following two verses: 1 Corinthians 6:18; 10:13.

It seems pretty clear from 1 Corinthians 6:18. Flee! Run away! When you are tempted sexually, run. When you are tempted, drawn back toward things you have struggled with in the past (whether that's addictions—substances or otherwise—or relationships), run. Your flesh is calling out to you, and it's not time to stand and fight. Remove yourself from the situation. Don't put yourself where you're likely to stumble.

We're called to run away in 1 Corinthians 10:13 as well. If God provides an escape, we should take Him up on it! He wouldn't provide us an escape route so we can stare at it. Run through it.

When have you needed to run from a tempting situation or person? Were you given a way out?

What time in your life did you decide not to run? What would a better, practical response have been?

Now you know the different situations that warrant different responses:

> God will fight our battles when we're discouraged and afraid.

> We should stand and fight when we are facing Satan and are under trials.

> We should flee when we're faced with temptation.

What situations are you facing in life right now? What response is needed?

LEADER GUIDE

OPENING AND CLOSING GROUP SESSIONS

Try to engage each student at the beginning of a group session. Once people begin to speak, even if only to answer a generic question, they are more likely to speak up later about more personal matters.

You may want to start each session by reviewing the previous week's personal study. This review provides context for the new session and opportunities to share relevant experiences, application, or truths learned between sessions. This would also be a good time to talk through your group's expectations for the coming week's study.

Always open and close the session with prayer, recognizing that only the Holy Spirit provides understanding and transformation in our lives. (The prayer suggestions provided in each session help focus members on Scripture, key truths, and personal application from the week's teaching.)

Remember that your goal isn't just meaningful discussion—it's discipleship.

WEEK 1: THE STRUGGLE IN EPHESUS

Getting Started (10 minutes)

> ⟩ Take a few minutes to go around the room and ask students to give their names and one word that they believe describes them. This may be particularly useful, because you may find out what students believe about their identity now.

> ⟩ Use the "Start" section on page 14 as a guide to engage students and get them talking and thinking about personal identity.

> As you lead students through these questions, be honest and authentic in your own answers. Your relationship with God isn't perfect and students need to see that. By talking through ways you're continually learning to obey, you create a safe place for students to share their struggles, fears, and ideas.

Watch (15-20 minutes)

> Watch the video for Session 1 (included in the DVD kit). On page 15, students will have space to take notes and fill in answers as they watch.

Discuss (25 minutes)

> Use the "Discuss" section on pages 16-17 to talk about the video with your group.

Before You Go (10 minutes)

> Take a minute to walk through "This Week's Plan," "Read", and "Reflect" with students. You can find a summary of each item on page 7. Encourage students to complete each of these on their own time throughout the coming week.

> Encourage students to find one person who will be their accountability partner throughout this study. If students need help finding a partner, consider placing them in pairs before your first meeting.

> Close by praying for your group. Use the guide on page 18 to pray specifically over issues you've touched on this week as you began your study of what it means to find your identity in Christ.

> Remind students to complete the Personal Studies on pages 22-29. As you complete these pages on your own, make sure to highlight and jot down insights you want to share with students in the next group session.

WEEK 2: NEW LIFE IN CHRIST

Getting Started (10 minutes)

> Use the "Start" section on page 32 as a guide to discuss last week's Personal Studies (pp. 22-29) and the "Reflect" section on page 21.

> Discuss how last week's memory verse, Ephesians 1:2, affected students.

> As you lead students through these questions, be honest and authentic in your own answers. Your answers not only help you connect with students, but also help them see how you're learning to apply new truths to your life as you walk through this study with them.

Watch (15-20 minutes)

> Watch the video for Session 2 (included in the DVD kit). On page 33, students will have space to take notes and fill in answers as they watch.

Discuss (25 minutes)

> Use the "Discuss" section on pages 34-35 to talk about the video with your group.

Before You Go (10 minutes)

> Encourage students to review "This Week's Plan" (p. 37) and complete the "Read" (p. 38) and "Reflect" (p. 39) activities.

> Suggest students continue meeting with their accountability partner throughout the study as they learn new information and apply it to their lives.

> Close by praying for your group. Use the guide on page 36 to pray specifically over issues you've touched on this week as you began your study of what it means to have new life in Christ.

> Remind students to complete the Personal Studies on pages 40-47. As you complete these pages on your own, make sure to highlight and jot down insights you want to share with students in the next group session.

WEEK 3: NEW LIFE IN COMMUNITY

Getting Started (10 minutes)

❭ Use the "Start" section on page 50 as a guide to discuss last week's Personal Studies (pp. 40-47) and the "Reflect" section on page 39.

❭ Ask students to describe any new insights they gained by reading through Ephesians 2 multiple times last week. Then, ask them to describe how they think this practice, reading Bible passages several times, will help them study God's Word in the future.

❭ As you lead students through these questions, be honest and authentic in your own answers. It will help students to know that others, even more mature believers, are still in the process of being transformed and struggle with living out the fruit of the Spirit.

Watch (15-20 minutes)

❭ Watch the video for Session 3 (included in the DVD kit). On page 51, students will have space to take notes and fill in answers as they watch.

Discuss (25 minutes)

❭ Use the "Discuss" section on pages 52-53 to talk about the video with your group.

Before You Go (10 minutes)

❭ Encourage students to review "This Week's Plan" (p. 55) and complete the "Read" (p. 56) and "Reflect" (p. 57) activities.

❭ Suggest students consider talking with their accountability partners about what this group and this relationship have given them a new outlook on community.

❭ Close by praying for your group. Use the guide on page 54 to pray specifically over issues you've touched on this week as you began your study of what it means to have new life in community.

> Remind students to complete the Personal Studies on pages 58-65. As you complete these pages on your own, make sure to highlight and jot down insights you want to share with students in the next group session.

WEEK 4: PURSUING UNITY IN CHRIST

Getting Started (10 minutes)

> Use the "Start" section on page 68 as a guide to discuss last week's Personal Studies (pp. 58-65) and the "Reflect" section on page 57.

> Invite students to share how the study "Are Small Groups Really That Important" (p. 58-61) inspired them to fully engage in this group and any other small groups they may be involved in.

> As you lead students through these questions, be honest and authentic in your own answers. As a leader, they will look up to you and follow your example when it comes to living in community.

Watch (15-20 minutes)

> Watch the video for Session 4 (included in the DVD kit). On page 69, students will have space to take notes and fill in answers as they watch.

Discuss (25 minutes)

> Use the "Discuss" section on pages 70-71 to talk about the video with your group.

Before You Go (10 minutes)

> Encourage students to review "This Week's Plan" (p. 73) and complete the "Read" (p. 74) and "Reflect" (p. 75) activities.

> Encourage students to discuss with their accountability partners the ways they specifically struggle to pursue unity with other believers. Clarify

that this does not give them permission to gossip about others, but to honestly share their own struggles and need for forgiveness.

〉 Close by praying for your group. Use the guide on page 72 to pray specifically over issues you've touched on this week as you began your study of what it means to pursue unity in Christ.

〉 Remind students to complete the Personal Studies on pages 76-83. As you complete these pages on your own, make sure to highlight and jot down insights you want to share with students in the next group session.

WEEK 5: PURSUING HOLINESS IN CHRIST

Getting Started (10 minutes)

〉 Use the "Start" section on page 86 as a guide to discuss last week's Personal Studies (pp. 76-83) and the "Reflect" section on page 75.

〉 Encourage students to share what they learned about their own spiritual gifts last week and how they might use them to serve others.

〉 As you lead students through these questions, be honest and authentic in your own answers. Help them understand that pursuing unity in Christ is a constant discipline and not a one-time deal.

Watch (15-20 minutes)

〉 Watch the video for Session 5 (included in the DVD kit). On page 87, students will have space to take notes and fill in answers as they watch.

Discuss (25 minutes)

〉 Use the "Discuss" section on pages 88-89 to talk about the video with your group.

Before You Go (10 minutes)

> Encourage students to review "This Week's Plan" (p. 91) and complete the "Read" (p. 92) and "Reflect" (p. 93) activities.

> As students meet with their accountability partners this week, ask them to consider confessing their sins to each other and praying over those specific struggles together.

> Close by praying for your group. Use the guide on page 90 to pray specifically over issues you've touched on this week as you began your study of what it means to pursue holiness.

> Remind students to complete the Personal Studies on pages 94-101. As you complete these pages on your own, make sure to highlight and jot down insights you want to share with students in the next group session.

WEEK 6: BE STRONG IN CHRIST

Getting Started (10 minutes)

> Take a minute to welcome students to the final group session of this study. Thank them for sticking with it throughout all six weeks. Consider bringing a gift or memento to help them remember who they are in Christ.

> Use the "Start" section on page 104 as a guide to discuss last week's Personal Studies (pp. 94-101) and the "Reflect" section on page 93.

> Ask students to talk about what God has called them to put off or put on this week, specifically.

> As you lead students through these questions, be honest and authentic in your own answers. Your students need a godly example of what it looks like to live in the light, even though we often make mistakes.

Watch (15-20 minutes)

> ❭ Watch the video for Session 6 (included in the DVD kit). On page 105, students will have space to take notes and fill in answers as they watch.

Discuss (25 minutes)

> ❭ Use the "Discuss" section on pages 106-107 to talk about the video with your group.

Before You Go (10 minutes)

> ❭ Encourage students to review "This Week's Plan" (p. 109) and complete the "Read" (p. 110) and "Reflect" (p. 111) activities.

> ❭ Ask students to spend time encouraging one another in their accountability groups and talking through ways they can continue to help each other stand strong in Christ, even after they complete the study at the end of this week.

> ❭ Close by praying for your group. Use the guide on page 108 to pray specifically over issues you've touched on this week as you began your study of what it means to be strong in Christ.

> ❭ Remind students to complete the Personal Studies on pages 112-119.

> ❭ Since you will not have a chance to review the Personal Studies, "Reflect" page, or guided reading from Session 6, consider hosting an optional seventh meeting (see pp. 128-129). If this is not possible, reach out to students and check-in with them to see if they have questions about the sixth session.

(OPTIONAL) WEEK 7: REVIEW

Getting Started (10 minutes)

› If you would like to meet with students once more to review the "Read" (p. 110), "Reflect" (p. 111), and Personal Study (p. 112-119) activities from week 6, consider hosting a seventh session at someone's home, grabbing dinner, going out for ice cream, or having a cookout if weather permits.

Review (35 minutes)

› Discuss last week's Personal Studies (pp. 112-119) and the "Reflect" section on page 111.

How have you learned to turn to God in the midst of challenges?

What did you learn about the importance of obeying your parents and how that relates to your relationship with God and others?

Who makes it possible for us to live in obedience?

How do you tell the difference between situations you should run away from and those you should stand and fight?

› Consider telling students a story from your own life about how obeying your parents (or disobeying them and facing the consequences) deeply affected you.

› As you lead students through these questions, be honest and authentic in your own answers. Consider sharing with students specific strategies you use or verses that help you to be strong in Christ.

Before You Go (10 minutes)

› Encourage students to stay in the Word and continue meeting with their accountability partners, even though the study has ended.

〉 Pray over your group. Ask God to help them remember all they have learned over the course of this study. Pray that He will strengthen them to continue to walk in His ways and give them wisdom as they apply what they have learned as we studied Ephesians together.

〉 Now, take some time to hang out with your group. Relax and spend time celebrating all that you learned and your hard work through the course of this study.

TIPS FOR LEADING A SMALL GROUP

PRAYERFULLY PREPARE

Prepare for each group session with prayer. Ask the Holy Spirit to work through you and the group discussion as you point to Jesus each week through God's Word.

REVIEW the weekly material and group questions ahead of time.

PRAY for each person in the group.

MINIMIZE DISTRACTIONS

Do everything in your ability to help students focus on what's most important: connecting with God, with the Bible, and with one another. Create a comfortable environment. If group members are uncomfortable, they'll be distracted and therefore not engaged in the group experience. Take into consideration seating, temperature, lighting, refreshments, surrounding noise, and general cleanliness.

Thoughtfulness and hospitality show guests and group members they're welcome and valued in whatever environment you choose to gather.

INCLUDE OTHERS

Your goal is to foster a community in which people are welcome just as they are but are also encouraged to grow spiritually. Always be aware of opportunities to include and invite new people.

INVITE new people to join your group.

INCLUDE anyone who visits the group.

ENCOURAGE DISCUSSION

A good small-group experience has the following characteristics.

EVERYONE PARTICIPATES. Encourage everyone to ask questions, share responses, or read aloud.

NO ONE DOMINATES—NOT EVEN THE LEADER. Be sure your time speaking as a leader takes up less than half your time together as a group. Politely guide discussion if anyone dominates.

NOBODY IS RUSHED THROUGH QUESTIONS. Don't feel that a moment of silence is a bad thing. People often need time to think about their responses to questions they've just heard or to gain courage to share what God is stirring in their hearts.

INPUT IS AFFIRMED AND FOLLOWED UP. Make sure you point out something true or helpful in a response. Don't just move on. Build community with follow-up questions, asking how other people have experienced similar things or how a truth has shaped their understanding of God and the Scripture you're studying. People are less likely to speak up if they fear that you don't actually want to hear their answers or that you're looking for only a certain answer.

GOD AND HIS WORD ARE CENTRAL. Opinions and experiences can be helpful, but God has given us the truth. Trust Scripture to be the authority and God's Spirit to work in people's lives. You can't change anyone, but God can. Continually point people to the Word and to active steps of faith.

KEEP CONNECTING. Think of ways to connect with group members during the week. Participation during the group session is always improved when members spend time connecting with one another outside the group sessions. The more people are comfortable with and involved in one another's lives, the more they'll look forward to being together. When people move beyond being friendly to truly being friends who form a community, they come to each session eager to engage instead of merely attending.

Encourage group members with thoughts, comments, or questions from the session by connecting through emails, texts, and social media.

Build deeper friendships by planning or spontaneously inviting group members to join you outside your regularly scheduled group time for meals; fun activities; and projects around your home, church, or community.

NOTES

NOTES

NOTES

NOTES

CHALLENGE CULTURAL IDENTITY STANDARDS

FOR GUYS!

FOR GIRLS!

Be A Man
John Paul Basham, General Editor

Be a Man is a seven-chapter study with contributions from some of the most notable voices in student ministry. *Be a Man* identifies and expands upon seven key aspects of discipleship that are essential to the spiritual development of any young man who longs to grow in Christ.

Salvage My Identity
Rachel Lovingood & Jennifer Mills

Salvaging My Identity is a 40-day, eight-chapter devotional experience for girls and young women that explores the spiritual restoration that takes place in every believer's life. *Salvaging My Identity* takes a biblical approach toward finding identity in Christ. Each chapter deals with common issues girls and young women face such as self-image, relationships, worldly influences, rejection, fear, and burnout.

TO LEARN MORE OR PURCHASE, VISIT LIFEWAY.COM OR VISIT YOUR LOCAL LIFEWAY CHRISTIAN STORE.